SECRETS of the BATTLEBOX

SECRETS of the BATTLEBOX

ROMEN BOSE

Marshall Cavendish
Editions

Picture Credits
Romen Bose: pg 29 (top), 32 (both), 46 (top), 50, 52, 54 (both), 59, 61, 65 (both), 128. The Imperial War Museum, London: pg 15, 71, 113, 114 and 131. By courtesy of The Straits Times with the permission of Singapore Press Holdings: Pg 24, 29 (bottom), 30, 44, 53, 56 and 57. By courtesy of the Battlebox: 46 (bottom), 124 (both). Map on page 98 reproduced from *The War in Malaya* published by Eyre and Spottiswoode. Every effort has been made to trace and credit the source of photographs and illustrations used. Please contact us if there have been any inadvertent errors or omissions.

Published by Marshall Cavendish Editions, reprinted 2011
An imprint of Marshall Cavendish International
1 New Industrial Road, Singapore 536196

Other Marshall Cavendish Offices
Marshall Cavendish Ltd. PO Box 65829, London EC1P 1NY, UK • Marshall Cavendish Corporation. 99 White Plains Road, Tarrytown NY 10591-9001, USA • Marshall Cavendish International (Thailand) Co Ltd. 253 Asoke, 12th Flr, Sukhumvit 21 Road, Klongtoey Nua, Wattana, Bangkok 10110, Thailand • Marshall Cavendish (Malaysia) Sdn Bhd, Times Subang, Lot 46, Subang Hi-Tech Industrial Park, Batu Tiga, 40000 Shah Alam, Selangor Darul Ehsan, Malaysia

Marshall Cavendish is a trademark of Times Publishing Limited

National Library Board Singapore Cataloguing in Publication Data
Bose, Romen.
Secrets of the battlebox : the history and role of Britain's command HQ during the Malayan campaign / Romen Bose. – Singapore : Marshall Cavendish Editions, 2011.
p. cm.
Includes bibliographical references.
ISBN : 978-981-4328-54-8

1. Great Britain – Armed Forces – Singapore – History. 2. World War, 1939-1945 – Campaigns – Malaysia – Malaya. I. Title.

UA649.32
940.5425 -- dc22   OCN665615445

Printed in Singapore by Fabulous Printers Pte Ltd

For Lara, Olive, Nisha and Anusha

May the lessons of the past
be a beacon to the future

Contents

Preface

This book that you hold in your hands would never have been possible had it not been for the long-suffering and continuing support of my wife Brigid, my daughters Lara and Olive as well as constant encouragement from my mum and dad.

The contents of this book are the result of 17 years of research into an area of Singapore's wartime history that has still not been investigated fully. With the death of so many of its participants and with most documents on the subject highly-classified and only recently open for research, there has been no opportunity till now to put forward the story of the Battlebox.

This book attempts to provide a very rough understanding to what the Battlebox was all about, its history, uses and final role in the Malayan Campaign. It attempts to address the gap in knowledge on one of the most crucial aspects of the Second World War in Malaya and Singapore, i.e. the role of the command headquarters, in the campaign.

There is very little in this book that is based on secondary sources as I took the decision from early on that this work would reflect the views and opinions of the participants in the events. As a result, it has a journalistic feel to it, where the main sources of reference and facts come from the participants as opposed to official histories and later interpretations of events.

I have also taken the liberty of dramatising the first chapter based on actual facts and recollections of the various actors and I hope this makes for easier reading and provides a better understanding of the material presented.

This book is aimed at those who want to know about the Battlebox and understand what actually happened there during the Malayan

Campaign. On another level, it also provides references and sources of information for those who want to do further research into the subject and will hopefully provide a good jumping off point for more work on this topic.

Although there are limited primary and secondary sources, there is still much to write on the command and communications structures of Malaya Command with repositories like the National Archives in London and Singapore, holding a wealth of documents relating to it.

I believe that history constantly evolves and a history that was written 10 years after an event will never be the same as that written 20, 30 or even 50 years later. With new documents released and different perspectives reflected, the revision of history provides us with a crucial understanding of how events are re-defined and viewed from even more differing perspectives, as more time passes. Although initial histories appear more visceral, later evaluations tend to provide a more considered perspective. However, both histories are essential if we are to understand what actually happened. With the death of the key participants, many of whom do not record their experiences, we are left only with secondary sources. For many areas of research, however, primary sources still do exist, in the form of memoirs, correspondence and reports, much of which have been filed away in the backrooms of archives waiting again to see the light of day.

I hope that I have provided many of these documents and in particular, introduced this subject to a new audience who will hopefully become more interested in the Second World War in Singapore.

Getting to the point of a final manuscript is never easy and I have to thank numerous individuals, who through their work and friendship, have contributed to this final version. I would like to single out Jeyathurai Ayadurai, managing director of the Singapore History Consultancy/ Journeys Pte Ltd, a very dear friend and military history buff, who has for long been encouraging me to get on with writing this book. Jeya, who lectured in Military History at the Singapore Command and Staff College for many years, before setting up his own company researching Singapore's history and carrying out tours based on it, has along with his right hand woman Savita Kashyap, developed an amazing walking tour of Fort Canning as part of the company's Battlefield Tour, which takes students and tourists alike on a dramatic adventure through the Battlebox and its surroundings. Jeya, along with his wife Jennifer, amazing administrator Ms Jeya and Savita, have for long been a bouncing board for my ideas and concepts regarding this period.

I must also thank Kwa Chong Guan, former director of the National Museum and presently Head of External Programs, Institute of Defence and Strategic Studies, Nanyang Technological University. His insights into the Battlebox have proven very useful and much credit must go to him and G. Uma Devi for their initial research on the Battlebox.

I have also benefited tremendously from the Reading Room at the Imperial War Museum, London, where staff at the Department of Records and Photographs have been of tremendous help. The National Army Museum in Chelsea was also of great help in providing personal diaries of soldiers who worked in the Battlebox prior to the fall. The National Archives (formerly the Public Records Office) in Kew was literally a treasure trove of documents and maps on the command headquarters, filling in large gaps in the puzzle that is the Battlebox.

This book would never had been possible had Faridah not brought me that first clipping in 1988 and much thanks go to Felix Soh, Iris, the late Teo Lian Huay, Glen, How San, the late R. Chandran, Alphonso Chan, G. Chandradas and Lee Ming Yen as well as the rest of the outstanding team at *The Straits Times.*

In conclusion, let me say that writing this book has been a labour of love and I remain solely responsible for any errors or mistakes within. Should you have comments on this book or if you have more information or leads for a future edition, please send me an email at romen@hotmail.com

Romen Bose
Summer 2005
London

Chapter 1

Introduction

Sunday, 15 February 1942.

The skies over the island of Singapore were overcast, filled with black smoke and fires, smoldering throughout the island. The constant sounds of explosions and air raid sirens filled the air.

The sun could not be seen for the large plumes of smoke from burning oil tanks, destroyed by the retreating military, obscuring most of the island's skyline.

On the streets, large numbers of exhausted and battle-weary troops filled the city, their faces covered in mud, soot and grime, their bodies unwashed for weeks, their will to fight completely destroyed. Many of their comrades had been killed in the preceding 70 days with even more captured as prisoners of the Imperial Japanese Army.

These men, who were resigned to the fate that awaited them, roamed the bombed-out streets that had already become the graveyard of numerous luxury cars and sedans, abandoned in the middle of roads and in alleyways by their fleeing European owners, many with keys still in their ignition. The cars and men were the only occupants of the streets as shops and offices were boarded up and shut without any sign of the local populace about. Everyone was in hiding as if in preparation for an impending storm or typhoon.

No one believed it would come to this. The proud subjects of a mighty British colony now hiding in terror as wave after wave of bombings scarred the city and where the smoke-laden air became too heavy even to breathe.

Singapore island had been shelled for the better part of a week with constant air raids over the city, decimating what remained of the civil services, with thousands of refugees fleeing from upcountry, filling burnt out buildings and huddled in slums throughout the city.

As the dull rays of the sun began to light the dawn, a tall, lanky figure in a sweat-drenched senior commander's khaki uniform stood on the balcony of his office on Fort Canning Hill, overlooking the burnt-out city and the chaos below.

There had been no sleep for a long, long time and there was to be no rest. He was tired, oh so very tired. All he wanted was sleep but sleep would not come. As his blood-shot eyes roamed the city, he took a slow drag from his umpteenth cigarette this hour, his thoughts wandering to England where his daughter, Dorinda, would be getting up in a few hours, celebrating her twelfth birthday with presents and cakes and parties.

There would be no presents and cakes and parties for him. He would not be there to share her joy or to help cut the cake, to lead the festivities. He knew now he might never ever see her again, as he and more than 100,000 men stood on the verge of destruction by a superior enemy.

"How had it all ended like this?" he wondered yet again as he walked into his office filled with the stale smell of too many cigarettes and sweat from too many huddled meetings.

It was barely six in the morning when he called his assistant from the outside office, telling him to arrange for a final meeting with everyone by nine in the morning. A decision would have to be made.

He washed his grimy and stubble-filled face in the bowl of brackish water, his only concession to his appearance. The taps had long since stopped working and all that was left was the water he had washed up in for the last four days. It didn't matter. None of this mattered any more. The battles had been lost one after the other and so many, many men had given their lives.

All that he had left now was his faith. But would that save him and his men? As he knelt down at the early morning communion service,

Lieutenant General Arthur Ernest Percival, General Officer Commanding, Headquarters Malaya Command, prayed that his men and the civilians caught in this bloody nightmare would survive the final onslaught of the Japanese Army that was sure to come in the next day or so.

The man who finally remained in charge of this shell-shocked and pockmarked island, Percival had withstood all that had been hurled at him and persevered, despite the massive blunders by senior and junior commanders and the lack of permission to carry out a real defence of the Malayan peninsula.

Here amidst the green and lush vegetation, which had been ripped up by heavy bombs and shelled with mortars, men from the headquarters, part of the remnants of the 100,000 strong British and Commonwealth military forces who had fought on the peninsula and had now retreated onto the island, gathered for prayers to sustain themselves for another day against an enemy that was about to overrun them.

Percival returned to his office, a colonial-styled building sitting on Fort Canning Hill. Located on Dobbie Rise, it was the nerve centre of Headquarters Malaya Command, where the military defence for Malaya and Singapore had been planned, executed and ultimately lost. Built in 1926, when British supremacy in the Far East was assured, the building had become, just like these final defenders of Singapore, an anachronism in the face of the new Japanese order in Malaya.

As he looked out across the balcony again, Ivan Simson, Chief Engineer and the Director General of Civil Defence walked in. The news overnight had been terrible. The water supply, Simson said, would not last another 24 hours. The food supplies, he was told, were expected to last another few days while ammunition was running

Lieutenant General A.E. Percival, General Officer Commanding, Headquarters Malaya Command

very low and the only petrol left was that in the fuel tanks of vehicles. All this, Percival noted studiously in his Hong Kong And Shanghai Bank bill folder; the final reports of a dead city. This bill folder would last the war and Percival's captivity, finally ending up in a box of personal papers at the Imperial War Museum in London, a long-forgotten testament to one of the lowest points in British military history.

Percival knew the time had come. The decision had to be made and made quickly. He picked up the telephone and waited to be connected. The military telephone exchange finally managed to get through on an external line. Most of the extensive telephone networks throughout Singapore and Malaya had been destroyed by the enemy. What remained barely worked. It was strange, Percival thought, that in order to make such a momentous decision, he would have to use a public telephone line to get hold of the one man who had the political power to make that decision.

That man was the Governor of the Straits Settlements, Sir Shenton Whitlegge Thomas. Thomas was responsible for Singapore and the Federated Malay States but it was the immense bureaucracy and red tape of the civil administration and their lack of willingness to prepare fully for war that led to the huge suffering of the local population and the total unpreparedness for the Japanese bombings and attacks.

Days before, the Governor had abandoned his residence at Government House and was squatting at the Singapore Club in the burnt out city. He had refused to make the decision when Percival and his senior Generals approached him in his new abode. He refused to meet with the Japanese nor would he respect their rule. He was the Governor, not a stooge of the Japanese. No, he would not surrender and he would not meet with them until they came and dragged him away.

On that fateful Sunday morning, the final logs from the switchboard at Fort Canning recorded that they were unable to raise the Governor. So it was that soon after the morning services and a short briefing by his chief engineer, Percival headed for a conference of his commanders, deep under the offices of Fort Canning, for another assessment of the situation.

Leaving his office, Percival made his way to the back of the command building. Under heavy camouflage, lay a small flight of stairs leading further up Fort Canning Hill. Percival, who was accompanied by Simson and his Administrative Adjutant Brigadier Lucas, walked up the short flight of stairs that led to an opening on the side of the hill.

Flanked by two huge metal doors and with a resonance of a deep rumbling coming from inside, Percival and his two senior officers walked in slowly. Where, only days ago, Sikh and Gurkha guards manned the entrance to this Top Secret inner sanctum of Malaya Command, with passwords and Secret clearances demanded of all who sought entrance, the doorway now laid empty with flickering lightbulbs illuminating the path into the warren of tunnels and rooms underneath.

The lack of guards showed the desperate plight of these last defenders of Singapore. All available troops had been drafted in the last line of defence against the enemy, a line that crumbled even before it was engaged by the enemy. Now there were no guards left to man the posts and it did not matter who sought entry. All was lost.

This was the fate of the Battlebox, Headquarters Malaya Command's state of the art Underground Communications Centre. Based on British Prime Minister Winston Churchill's own Cabinet War Rooms, from where the Battle of Britain and the battles of World War II were planned and fought, the Battlebox was supposed to provide British and Allied forces in Malaya and Singapore a unified command centre from which to defend and strike against the invading Japanese army. Instead, it would now mark the end of British dominance in Southeast Asia.

Percival entered a blistering inferno of heat as the ventilation system had broken down with the cut in power supply. The back up generators were insufficient to the task and so the entrances to the bunkers were left open at all times and could not be closed even during bombing raids as the air would then be unbreathable.

With more than 500 officers and men working feverishly in the 30-room Battlebox, the rooms were filled with the all too familiar sour smell of sweat and stale cigarette smoke. A constant stench also permeated the rooms as the latrines had broken down from being overloaded and there were no troops around who could fix them.

Percival walked by the chaos in the Gun Operations Room. Sector after sector had been conceded to the enemy even as late as 14 February, with most remaining battalions in tatters and communications cut off to most major units on the island. The faces of exhausted and demoralised staff officers greeted Percival as he looked at the plotting table.

As he looked over the final dispositions of troops, Percival received an urgent communiqué from the Signals Control Room. The highly secret teletyped sheet was final permission from General Sir Archibald Wavell, Supreme Commander of the American, British, Dutch and Australian Command to capitulate the Allied forces in the worst case.

The Most Secret message read:

> So long as you are in a position to inflict losses and damage to the enemy and your troops are physically able to do so you must fight on. Time gained and damage to enemy are of vital importance at this crisis. When you are fully satisfied that this is no longer possible I give you discretion to cease resistance. Before doing so all arms, equipment and transport of value to enemy must of course be rendered useless. Also just before final cessation of fighting opportunities should be given to any determined bodies of men or individuals to try and effect escape by any means possible. They must be armed. Inform me of intentions. Whatever happens I thank you and all troops for your gallant efforts of last few days.[1]

He read it carefully, then folded the sheet and put it in his pocket. He would now have to make the decision. He was finally given the permission to surrender all British and Allied forces as well as the civilian government.

If only they had given him and earlier General Officers Commanding in Malaya similar permission years before, to fight the enemy with the various services and the civilian government under his authority, things might have been very different. At the start of the War, he only had control over the army, while the air force and navy were instructed by their own service chiefs. He had no control over the bureaucratic red tape in the civil administration and even at times, what the Australian and Indian troops were doing under their various commanders.

By 9:30am, most of the senior commanders had gathered in the room of the Commander, Anti-Aircraft Defences, Brigadier A.W.G. Wildey. Wildey had been made responsible for up to the minute movements of the Japanese forces, which were being plotted out of the Gun Operations Room next door.

It was a very small and stuffy room, filled with pipes from the emergency generators set up once the power supply to the Battlebox had been cut. The atmosphere in the room was tense and the smell of defeat permeated the air as further reports of casualties and retreats trickled in.

Percival walked in with Simson and Wildey, who took their seats next to him. Seated already were Lieutenant General Sir Lewis Heath, General Officer Commanding the III Indian Corps, Major-General Gordon Bennett, Commander of the 8th Australian Division, Brigadier T.K. Newbigging, Brigadier K.S. Torrance and several other senior officers.

The only junior officer present was Major C.H.D. Wild, a staff officer from the III Indian Corps and one of the few officers remaining who was fluent in Japanese.

Major Wild, who came to play a key role in prosecuting the Japanese for war crimes after the war, described what happened in that small, stiflingly hot room.

> ... Between 0900 and 0930hrs on 15 Feb '42 I accompanied the Corps Commander in my capacity as his GSO2(O) to the final conference in the underground "Battlebox" at Fort Canning. Lt.Gen. A.E. Percival invited a review of the situation from the senior officers present. I recall in particular that the C.E. (Chief Engineer) Brigadier Simson said that no more water would be available in Singapore from some time during the next day (16 Feb): also that the C.R.A. (Chief of Royal Artillery, Brigadier E.W. Goodman, 9th Indian Division) said that Bofors ammunition would be exhausted by that afternoon (15 Feb), and that another class of ammunition, either 18pdr or 25pdr, was likewise practically exhausted. The decision to ask for terms was taken without a dissentient voice. Some minutes later, when details of the surrender were being discussed, Major General Gordon Bennett, GOC 8th Aust Div, remarked "How about a combined counter-attack to recapture Bukit Timah?" This remark came so late, as was by then so irrelevant, that I formed the impression at the time that it was made not as a serious contribution to the discussion but as something to quote afterwards. It was received in silence and the discussion proceeded. [2]

It is interesting that in the official minutes of this meeting, written in captivity and which survived the war, it was noted that Percival asked about a combined counter-attack. There was no mention of Bennett's comment.

It was clear that the various commanders were all in favour of surrender but that it was Percival who would have to make the final decision.

When he asked General Heath for his opinion on the best course to adopt, the commander of the III Indian Corps, was acerbic. "In my opinion there is only one possible course to adopt and that is to do what you ought to have done two days ago, namely to surrender immediately" [3]

In the final stage of the meeting, there could have been no doubt as to what the decision would be.

Based on the water shortage, the demoralised troops, his commander's unanimous decision to surrender and with the final permission from Wavell in his pocket, Percival could now capitulate without the loss of more troops and the death of huge numbers of civilians should the Japanese attack Singapore town. For being forced to make the decision to surrender, the blame of the fall of Singapore would forever more fall upon his shoulders, whether it was deserved or not.

The official minutes recorded dryly,

> "The G.O.C., in view of the critical water situation and the unsatisfactory administrative situation generally, thereupon reluctantly decided to accept the advice of the senior officers present and to capitulate." [4]

Hostilities would cease at 1630hrs GMT with a deputation sent to meet the Japanese as outlined in flyers dropped by the Japanese air force all over Singapore days before.

Once the conference terminated at 11:15am, Percival headed to the Signals Control Room, where he drafted his last message to Wavell:

> "Owing to losses from enemy action water petrol food and ammunition practically finished. Unable therefore continue the fight any longer. All ranks have done their best and grateful for your help." [5]

Throughout the rest of the day, Percival was listless. Once the decision had been made, orders had been given to destroy everything. With the last message sent to Wavell, instructions were given to destroy all the cipher and code books. Brigadier Lucas also ordered all signal equipment to be smashed up.

As this began, calls continued to come in from units all over the island for instructions. The officers at the Battlebox had none. In the afternoon and evening, there were bonfires outside the Battlebox as secret documents and files were burnt in order to prevent them from falling into enemy hands. However, much of the equipment and infrastructure in the Battlebox was left intact.

What transpired later that afternoon is well documented in history books as Percival signed the surrender document handing over the British and Commonwealth forces under his command to Lieutenant General Tomoyuki Yamashita, Commander of the Japanese 25th Army, ending 70 days of fighting down the Malayan peninsula leading to the inglorious surrender at the Ford Motor Factory in Bukit Timah.

Much has been written on the fall of Singapore and the last hours and days of the British command as they agonised over the final surrender to the Japanese but very little has been recorded of what went on within the walls of the Battlebox and Percival's war rooms as well as the conditions that the officers and men of the Battlebox worked under. Many of these officers and men are now long gone, more than 60 years after the end of the Second World War.

What remains, however, are the rooms where these most difficult of decisions were made.

The history of the Battlebox and its surroundings as well as of the combined headquarters of the British and commonwealth forces during the War in Malaya still remains shrouded in mystery. They were kept very secret to prevent the enemy from destroying these complex nerve centres of military operations. Even before surrender, many of the records detailing the goings-on in the Battlebox were destroyed with no traces left.

Many who died in Japanese prisoner of war camps took the remaining secrets of these facilities with them to the grave, and those who survived have passed on in recent years make it difficult to piece together the full use and historical events that these bunkers saw. Thus, some of the events above and in this book have been extrapolated and re-created through extensive research and analysis, in order to link the various pieces of the secret puzzle and form part of the real story of what took place at the Battlebox.

In the chapters ahead, from recently declassified documents, numerous interviews, secret sources and over 17 years of in-depth investigations, you will read about the building of this long forgotten underground communications centre, its nooks and crannies, how it was utilised in the Malayan campaign and its role in the final days of the battle for Singapore.

For the first time ever, the secrets of the Battlebox will be revealed, like the location of the Allied combined headquarters of the army and air force in Sime Road and the post-war history of these complexes that remain a historical legacy of the last world war.

Secrets of the Battlebox will shed much more light on what happened in the Malayan Campaign and in the deep dark rooms under Fort Canning Hill, rooms in which the future of Singapore and Malaysia were decided. Rooms, that even today, have an uncomfortable resonance of a not too distant past.

Endnotes

1   Churchill, W.S. *The Second World War: The Hinge of Fate*. Houghton Mifflin Company, Boston, USA, 1950. p. 104.

2   Wild, C.H.D. *Note on the Capitulation of Singapore*. Unpublished typescript. New Delhi, India, 30 November 1945. p. 2.

3   *Proceedings of the Conference held at Headquarters Malaya Command (Fort Canning) at 0930Hrs. Sun. 15 February 1942, Papers of A.E. Percival, P16-27.* The Imperial War Museum, London, p. 2.

4   Ibid, p. 3.

5   Churchill, W.S. *The Second World War: The Hinge of Fate*. Houghton Mifflin Company, Boston, USA, 1950. p. 105.

Chapter 2

The Discovery

It was the middle of July 1988 when I walked in to the newsroom at *The Straits Times*, Singapore's oldest daily, then located at Kim Seng Road.

Two weeks into a summer internship working on the General Desk at the renowned newspaper, I was relishing the fact that although only eighteen and in university, I was able to rub shoulders with some of the best veteran journalists in the trade.

So a few weeks into my internship, when I was approached by Faridah, assistant to then General Desk Editor Felix Soh, I thought I was going to get a big break.

To my disappointment, she presented me with a Forum page letter printed in the newspaper days earlier and told me that Felix wanted me to follow it up.

The letter, by Doraisingam Samuel, a former president of the Singapore History Association, claimed the existence of an underground bunker complex under Fort Canning Park in downtown Singapore. The bunker, he said, had been used by the British in 1942 during the Second World War and Samuel wanted the Parks and Recreation Department to open it and turn it into a museum.

"Oh boy," I thought to myself. Just another weak lead to follow up on, one which would most probably not pan out as there was obviously no such thing as a bunker under Fort Canning. If there were, surely we would all have known about it by now.

Yet another historical mystery that would never be solved just like the rumours of "hidden Japanese gold" claimed to have been secretly buried by Japanese soldiers in the Philippines and Thailand at the end of the War.

I made the requisite calls to get hold of Mr. Samuel but was unable to reach him. I went down to the newspaper library and searched through all the files we had on the Malayan Campaign and Fort Canning but there was no mention of any bunker or underground complex.

It seemed a hopeless task to be able to dig any deeper and even my letter to the British High Commission's Defence Advisor turned up nothing. I was later to learn that even the High Commission had no clue as to the existence of the Battlebox.

Just when I was about to give up on it all, Felix called me over to his desk.

A veteran newspaperman, Felix had worked with many newspapers in his career before joining *The Straits Times* as the very dynamic editor of the General Desk. His inspiration and energy carried most of us on, even when we didn't want to go on. He did not suffer fools gladly and many were the days when I would get an earful for submitting substandard copy or committing some grammatical or stylistic faux pas. The other interns and I were terrified of him and with good reason.

On that day, Felix was in his element. There had been several major scoops the day before and many compliments on how well the General Desk was performing. When I gave him my report, he looked thoughtful and then gave me the lead that would break open the story.

It was a picture of the outside of the alleged "tunnel complex" at Fort Canning that was opened by Civil Defence officers just months before in February 1988 and was only briefly examined before being sealed up by the Parks and Recreation Department.

The picture had been published in the Chinese language papers and promptly forgotten. No mention of it had been made in *The Straits Times* or anywhere else.

I was intrigued. So was there really an underground bunker like the one Churchill used, a cabinet war rooms of sorts in Singapore? I had to find out more and I called up Mr. Kwa Chong Guan, then director of the Singapore Oral History Department, who was named in the photo caption as one of the key persons involved in the February opening.

A distinguished scholar, who had researched Singapore's early history and that of Fort Canning, Kwa would later head the National Museum. He and his team were in the midst of trying to discover the secret history of this underground complex which I had yet to see for myself. Kwa along with John Miksic, an archeologist and lecturer at the National University of Singapore, had instigated the February opening of the bunker.

Kwa and Miksic said at that point, only a handful of people had made it briefly into the complex and a full investigation had yet to take place.

But it was clear from Kwa's initial research that this was where General Percival held his last meeting with senior commanders before surrendering Singapore and 100,000 British and Commonwealth troops to the Japanese.

A picture of the initial opening of the bunker on 22 February 1988, with Kwa Chong Guan and John Miksic standing to the extreme right of the picture. Singapore Civil Defence officers can be seen ventilating the complex. The bunker was only cursorily examined before being "sealed up" again.

My first question to Kwa was who was this Percival? And what was so significant about this underground tunnel?

Up until the early 1990s, secondary school students in Singapore, who did not take history up to Secondary Four level, were only exposed to two years of history lessons which covered ancient history in the near and far east but nothing about the 20th century in Southeast Asia. I had known from elderly relatives that Singapore had suffered during the War but not much more. Kwa and his senior researcher G. Uma Devi gave me a quick history lesson on the Second World War in Singapore.

At the end of it, Kwa said it was unclear when exactly the bunkers were built but confirmed that there definitely were bunkers, a huge complex of rooms that were sealed up since the late 1960s.

Although information on the Battlebox was scarce, Kwa was able to locate a blueprint of the bunker complex, in the Land Office at Singapore's Law Ministry. He had made enquiries in London and at the National Archives in Singapore but to no avail. It was the Law Ministry that finally located a copy of the blueprint which was handed over to the Oral History Department.

In addition, he showed me numerous maps of Fort Canning from the turn of the century when an actual fort was located on the hill, with gun redoubts and a moat!

From the minutes of meetings among papers donated by Percival to the Imperial War Museum in London and documents from the historian Louis Allen, a rough picture began to emerge of the use of the Battlebox and the last days of Headquarters Malaya Command.

Kwa and his team had done an enormous amount of research in the hopes that the information would convince the authorities to preserve the Battlebox for future generations.

Could it be that such an interesting campaign and the building of such a highly sensitive structure occurred in this country less than 50 years ago? That night I got hold of a copy of Noel Barber's classic work on the fall of Singapore, *Sinister Twilight*, and began boning up on the Malayan Campaign.

The next day, I told Felix that we were on to one of the most exciting historical sites in the history of the Malayan Campaign! I was thrilled to finally sink my teeth into what was becoming a very exciting story indeed!

"This is the kind of excitement I like to see in a journalist", he said grinning. "But, you must make sure that you have the full story, from all angles. I want quotes from the authorities and the historians and an explanation of what actually happened 46 years ago. And I want it quick before anyone else gets this story."

I was impressed that Felix let me run with the story instead of putting a seasoned journalist on it. He knew it was my scoop and made sure I would break it when the time came.

But what I needed to do next was to see the bunkers for myself. That would be the most exciting part of this assignment.

From a copy of the blueprint that Kwa lent me, it was obvious that the bunker was large and that without actually walking through the complex, it would be impossible to write about it.

So I called up the National Parks Department, which was in charge of the Fort Canning Park and the bunkers within it, to get permission to go into the Battlebox. But the officials there refused to let me view the complex as it was "dirty and hot and was not safe for entry. Moreover, the entrance had been sealed!"

I was thoroughly disappointed. For days, I tried to get permission to go in and for days the department had been indecisive on what to do and had referred my request to higher authorities.

Finally, in frustration, I decided to take things into my own hands and go down to Fort Canning to see what was actually there.

I needed a photographer and as luck would have it, the Photo Desk was keen to send out a rookie photographer who had joined the paper after serving in the military. The photographer, whom I shall call Al, to protect his identity, was young, idealistic and very, very gung-ho.

I decided that if the entrance had been sealed and we couldn't get in through the doors, what about trying to sneak in through vents on the blueprint that appeared to lead directly into the complex? This would mean I would get an exclusive scoop on the bunker which was now being talked about in historical circles around town.

Al was quick to agree when he heard my plans as it clearly sounded like the beginnings of an exciting adventure.

So the next day, we took a quick cab ride from Times House to Fort Canning and stood at the foot of the bunker on Cox Terrace as a thick canopy of trees covered the entire area in a surreal greenish light, with the chirping of cicadas our only company in the jungle-like surroundings.

We looked all round for the vents on the side of the hill where the bunker was supposed to be located but all we could find was a disused children's playground on the top of the hill and these odd-looking mushroom shaped concrete structures. I then realised that the mushroom structures were the roofs of the vents which had been sealed on all sides to prevent nosy people like me from gaining access.

I sat next to the playground located directly above the bunker and was pondering how to proceed with my story without having any chance to see the inside.

Al then called me over to the other side of the bunker on the Dobbie Rise side of the hill. He pointed out a door in a wall that jutted out slightly and looked like a storage shed from the outside. Al asked whether this might be the entrance but I told him that the Parks Department said the entrance had been sealed so the door most probably led to a storage shed.

From his experience in the military, Al did not look convinced. "It's a strange looking storage shed which has a ventilation shaft right on top of it", he said. How could it be that a storage room would have a ventilation shaft right on top unless it led to something? But the Parks and Recreation Department said they had sealed the entrance so how come there was a door here? Could they have overlooked this door? It had been padlocked but the lock used was very flimsy.

As Al and I were tugging to see whether the lock would budge, it suddenly broke. I was now in a quandary. Should I open the door and go in and find out what was in the room? If my hunch was right, it would lead to the huge bunker complex which would earn me my first ever scoop. Should I stay outside and not enter a place that was clearly

The only identifiable signs of the Battlebox from the top of Fort Canning Hill, the concrete mushroom-like structures formed the top of the ventilation systems operating in the complex below. The mushrooms still remain in the park, in addition to a new structure above the emergency rooftop exit. In the background is the former barracks on Cox Terrace. It has now been converted into an arts centre and a culinary cuisine institute.

The locked door on the Dobbie Rise side of the bunker, before the lock accidentally fell apart. It could easily be mistaken for a storage shed. Note how close it is to the main road on Dobbie Rise and the drainage ditch dug in front of the doorway.

sealed off and not meant for trespass? Going in could also mean that we would get lost or even prosecuted for entering a restricted facility!

It was a very long 10 seconds as my journalistic instincts got into gear and I dived in with Al in tow into a musty smelling chamber. On entering, the darkness enveloped me and the musty air made me cough. We walked in further and a short staircase led up and down again until we were in a long corridor which was only brightened by the flashlights we had brought along.

I recorded the adventure in a notebook I had brought along.

Inside it was extremely humid and very hot even though the complex was located so deep under the hill.

The bunker was totally dilapidated with wires hanging from the walls and the rooms were flooded with two to three inches of water.

Just below the entrance, we spotted a wrecked scooter. Discoloured and rusty, it was a relic from the 40s or 50s. Ironically, wordings were penned on the bike which said, "Do Not Remove", and there it remained,

The rusted motorcycle in the bunker. Just above the rear tyre, the words, "Do Not Remove" were scribbled on. No one had moved it for more than 20 years by the time we found it in 1988.

for the last thirty to forty years, lying in situ until we happened upon it. I wonder whatever happened to that relic of the bunker?

Further down the passage, we spotted a doorway labeled, "Air Filtration Plant". Inside, what remained was just a shell of the machine, with its ducts all rusty and stained.

The metal doors throughout the complex were all rusted and several were falling off their hinges. Surprisingly, we found ceramic washbasins with taps intact inside some of the rooms. Most of the metal pieces and wiring had been stripped clean by looters, including light switches and furniture. All the rooms were completely stripped of any moveable objects.

In the "G" Clerks room, we found an empty stretcher that had been abandoned on the floor and decomposing in the heat and humidity of the place. It looked bloodstained but it was hard to tell 40 years on. It was eerie to see a stretcher lying in the middle of a dark empty room and I felt a cold chill run down the back of my neck. We decided not to tarry any longer and quickened our pace.

There were also toilets in the bunker. The urinals were yellowed with age and we found a light bulb at the bottom of one. The toilet bowls were no better for we found a door stuck into one and the toilet seats and walls filled with fungus growth.

Power and light sockets were also stripped and rotten planks were strewn all over the place. The clay floor tiles had begun to dissolve in the various flooded rooms, which appeared to have been waterlogged for decades. This meant that we ended up getting stuck in the wet muck every time we took a step forward. It was hard moving and we realised that it would be easier to walk on any dry spots where the tiles had not dissolved. We found lots of tiles stacked in corners and when I lifted one, it crumbled in my hands.

We also found the remains of a dog, most probably lost in the maze of rooms in the bunker. It had died of starvation or sickness, its bones a reminder not to stray too far away from the entrance.

The room labeled, "Fortress Plotting Room", had large parts of its floor dug out and a huge pile of dirt lay exposed on the side. The walls were covered with cork boards, obviously used for hanging maps and charts on the walls.

The toilet bowl. The seats showed signs of decay with fungus growth and the bowl was badly discoloured.

One of the few items left intact in the Battlebox, this washbasin was located in the Fortress Plotting Room.

We also found several artifacts including a penknife, a spanner and a pair of pliers in the bunker and in the process, located another two sealed entrances into the bunker (Cox Terrace side and roof entrance).

There was also a metal plank standing vertically, with what seemed like red stains on it and the walls which were covered with dangling wires were also dirtied, stained and marked with unidentifiable graffiti.

That was enough adventure and mustiness for one day as Al shot at least ten rolls of film in the bunker complex itself.

We were hot, sticky and our shoes filled with soft muddy clay from the terracotta tiles that lined the floors in the bunker. The water was believed to have been rain which came in from the vents and rooftop entrances in the decade that it was abandoned before the complex was finally sealed off.

Weary after our afternoon's adventure, I was now terrified. How was I going to explain to Felix what I had done in order to get the pictures for the story and to view the complex for myself?

It took a lot of nerve to walk up to him that afternoon and tell him what I had just done.

Felix hit the roof!

After an hour of being bawled out for such unprofessional behaviour and for jeopardising our lives, he calmed down. On the inside, he was thrilled that we had the pictures and the potential for a big scoop. On the outside, he had to set rules for these journalists who had flouted the law.

I was slightly ashamed but knew that we had a good story. However, as a result of the risk we took, I could have done much damage to the reputation of the paper and to myself. After the scolding and my promise not to do something like that again, Felix let us off, saying, "when I say take the initiative, I don't mean breaking and entering!"

"You two are the craziest reporters I know and I must make sure not to send the two of you out together on any other assignments", he said.

For the next few months, almost every assignment I covered was with Al!

But we still had a dilemma. In order to use the pictures, we had to get permission to go into the bunker officially and do it by the book this time. Otherwise, it would be impossible to publish the story or the pictures we had in our hands.

Again, I called the Parks Department and again they demurred. When I spoke to the senior official in charge and told him there was a door to the bunker and that it was not sealed up, he was very surprised.

If we hadn't been down to the bunker we would not have known of the existence of the door. The presence of a door meant we could go in as there was no resealed wall that would have to be broken.

It transpired that the Public Works Department (PWD), who had been involved in the February opening, felt that it would be better to put a door to the entrance rather than seal it off again for easy re-entry so they had installed a door just days after the initial reopening of the bunker by the Parks Department.

Although we even managed to get the Singapore Civil Defence Force (SCDF) from Nee Soon Camp to agree to come down and ventilate the bunkers before we went it, permission was still not forthcoming until Felix got on the line with the officials.

It seemed that they were planning a big launch of the Bunker's discovery and *The Straits Times* story would steal the thunder from their press conference in a few months time.

Felix told them that the cat was already out of the bag and it was better to cooperate on this story so that we could publish the full picture which would then benefit everyone.

After much cajoling, the Parks Department became one of our biggest champions in making sure the story was told. Permission was quickly granted and on 23 July, together with the SCDF and S.C. Wong, a technical officer from the Public Works Department, we "officially" went into the bunker.

On arrival at the bunker, officials from the PWD were curious as to why the door was unlocked but assumed that the flimsy lock must have been removed by vandals.

Al and I didn't say a word. A few days later a new lock similar to the old one, anonymously donated, appeared next to the entrance.

Once inside the Battlebox, we documented the place thoroughly and today, the large number of photographs as to what the complex looked like when it was reopened remains in *The Straits Times* photo library for use by future historians and researchers.

My exclusive story on the bunker and its history appeared in *The Straits Times* on 26 July 1988, a scoop that was the talk of the town for the next few days.

But for me, the story didn't just end there. The introduction to the history of Singapore and the secrets of the Battlebox lit a flame within me.

It inspired me to finally do a honours degree in modern Southeast Asian history in addition to a finance degree as well as making numerous trips in the intervening years to the Imperial War Museum, National Army Museum and the Public Records Office in the UK.

The article which appeared in The Straits Times *on 26 July 1988 highlighting the discovery of the long forgotten Battlebox.*

The past 17 years have been spent in researching and understanding the history of the Battlebox and the role it had played in the War in Malaya.

I had co-authored a book on World War II battlefield sites in Singapore and written another on the Indian Independence Movement in Singapore during the Second World War. As a former Bureau Chief and correspondent, I had also produced historical documentaries on the Second World War and news reports on events marking the period.

As a result of my ongoing in-depth research into the Battlebox and Singapore's World War II history, I had accumulated so much material on the Battlebox that I decided to put it all in a book. So, more than 17 years after I first set foot in the Battlebox, I have finally managed to pen down a history of this amazing complex.

Today, the Battlebox has been converted into a first-rate museum with interesting displays and animatronics to highlight what happened in Singapore and Malaya during and after the campaign. The complex has been converted to educating the young on the mistakes of the past and the opportunities for the future. A trip to the Battlebox is a must for anyone who wants a quick lesson on Singapore's wartime history.

In the next chapter, you will read about how the Battlebox came about and what its various rooms were used for and more importantly, how it faced up to the challenge of the War in Malaya.

Chapter 3

The Underground Command Centre

The Underground Command Centre or Battlebox lies under one of the first hills occupied by the British East India Company after Sir Stamford Raffles landed at the tiny fishing village of Singapore in 1819.

Known as Bukit Larangan or Forbidden Hill to the Malay, Chinese and Indian villagers who lived on the island, the hill was the sacred burial ground of past Malay kings and rulers. People were forbidden from going up the hill, which may have also served as private residences for earlier Sultans and Kings. Today, the Keramat of Sultan Iskandar Shah remains one of the only visible marks of ancient burials, the site reputed to be the resting place of the last ruler of 14th Century Singapore and the founder of the Malacca Sultanate.

According to Colonel L.T. Firbank in his *History of Fort Canning*:

> By... 1 April 1819... Already a settlement was spreading over the Plain—lines for the troops at the foot of the hill, bazaar and followers quarters. The hill at the back, Bukit Larangan, now Fort Canning, had been cleared of trees, and Lieutenant Ralfe of the H.E.I. Company's Artillery, who had been appointed the first Executive Engineer, had laid a road around it (the beginnings of what is now Canning Rise, leading from Coleman Street).[1]

The earliest known sketch of Singapore town, which dates from 1823, showed the town southeast of Bukit Larangan and northeast of the Singapore River.

In sketches of the town from that period the central background shows Bukit Larangan, which was also known as Government Hill from 1822 to 1859 before it was renamed Fort Canning Hill. The house near the summit, close to the flagstaff, was the bungalow built for Raffles during his third visit to Singapore, which he mentions in a letter to his friend William Marsden:

> We have lately built a small bungalow on Singapore Hill where though the height is inconsiderable, we find a great difference in climate. Nothing can be more interesting and beautiful than the view from this spot... The tombs of the Malay Kings are close at hand, and I have settled that if it is my fate to die here I shall take my place amongst them: this will at any rate be better than leaving my bones at Bencoolen... [2]

The house was subsequently purchased by the British government and in 1826 its cost stood on the books as $916. In 1823, the Second Resident of Singapore, John Crawford, expanded and improved the house at his own expense although he did receive $150 monthly as a housing allowance.

Raffles' house remained on Fort Canning as the residence of the Resident Councillor and eventually the newly appointed Governor until it was taken over by the military in 1858.

At that point, the Governor was provided with a rented residence at the Pavilion, a house formerly occupying the top of Oxley Hill, for six months while the owner was on leave in Europe.

From 1859 to 1869, Colonel Orfeur Cavenagh (Governor 1861-67) and then Colonel Harry St George Ord (Governor 1867-73) lived in the old Leonie Hill House, off Grange Road, until Government House (the Istana) was ready for occupation.

By May 1859, Government Hill had been converted into a new strongly defended position called Fort Canning, named after Lord Canning the Governor General and first Viceroy of India. Seven acres at the top of the hill were levelled and seven 68-pounder guns were mounted in the field redoubts on the southern end, facing the Straits.

Eventually, more that 17 pieces of artillery were mounted. However, by 1892, the Fort was no longer considered effective and remained as a barracks for the garrison artillery and as the general signal station for the town. It fired salutes and time guns at 5am, noon and 9pm but no longer had any value as a defensive position with many other new forts and batteries set up to defend the Straits and Singapore town.[3]

The history of Fort Canning moving into the twentieth century remains sketchy at best but we do know that the Fort finally made way for Singapore's first underground reservoir located on the top of the hill.

By this time, the military forces on the island had been reinforced with the decision to build a great naval base in Singapore.

It was seen in reports as, "the most secure base south of Hong Kong" and its hinterland was more firmly under British control than Hong Kong's. More importantly, this port stood at the western gateway of the Pacific, and occupied "to the British Empire in the East a corresponding position to Gibraltar in the West"

The sum of £63 million would finally be spent in a stop-start building programme that eventually saw the huge naval base in Sembawang completed by February 1938.

But by then, the prospect of war with Japan became a reality with the Japanese invasion of Manchuria and with a large amount of espionage being carried out by a network of Japanese spies throughout the Malayan peninsula.

The British strategy to defend Singapore meant that there was a need for a significant number of soldiers, airmen and sailors to fully defend the newly built base and numbers were gradually increased in the 1930s. What was also crucial was the setting up of a proper headquarters for all British and Commonwealth forces, with the main headquarters of Malaya Command being Singapore.

However, as all three services operated under separate instructions from London, three independent service headquarters were set up. The navy would operate from the brand new naval base while the air force was located at Seletar, and the army was by now based at Fort Canning.

Although the army and air force finally did set up a combined operations room at Sime Road before the war began, it proved to be very problematic. More on this in Chapter 5.

But in 1936, General Percival, General Officer Commanding, Malaya Command, noted that:

> ... the idea of the operational staffs of the fighting services working together had begun to take shape in the plans for the bomb-proof headquarters at Fort Canning.[4]

The underground command centre was thus built to house not only the operational staff of the services but also allied representatives of the French, Dutch and the Americans. Rooms were allocated to these forces in the initial blueprints for the Battlebox.

The 29 rooms built into the hill just next to the covered reservoir measured 44 metres by 48.6 metres and were located 9.1 metres below the tennis courts and club house nearby.

The whole area remained camouflaged so that from the air, the top of the hill appeared to be just an area of green surrounded by the command buildings on Dobbie Rise and barracks blocks on Cox Terrace.

Before proceeding, there are a few things that need to be explained.

Much of the information and detail on the Battlebox that you will read from here on has never been made public. Culled from top secret and highly sensitive war-time documents that have only recently been declassified by the British government and from numerous sources, who even today, wish to remain anonymous, the picture that emerges of the rooms and chambers that make up the Battlebox is quite amazing. Some of the descriptions you will read also come from a bound set of anonymous research clippings and interviews compiled by the Singapore Oral History Department and Parks and Recreation Department.

However, even with these clippings and over 17 years of continuous in-depth research into numerous archives in Singapore and the UK as well as several exploratory trips to the underground complex, the Battlebox has yet to reveal all of its secrets and there is much of the puzzle that has yet to be solved.

However, the details that have emerged provide a vivid picture of the role played by the various elements of Headquarters Malaya Command, housed in the rooms of the Battlebox, as the British military fought the advancing Japanese forces from northern Malaya all the way to the docks of Singapore Harbour, in less than 70 days.

I have also modified the original blueprint to reflect the various doorways and wall positions in the rooms as they were when the Battlebox was unsealed in 1988. Thus, the blueprint shows the most accurate layout of the bunkers as they were in February 1942 as opposed to the modified rooms and layout of the Battlebox Museum today.

From the blueprint, it can be seen that there are two main entrances and an emergency roof exit, whose existence was a closely guarded secret.

I have followed the number sequence as originally listed above the doorways of the rooms, many of which are still visible today. For those rooms that are not numbered and for which we have no information, I have left blank in the hopes that sometime in the future information may emerge to help us fill in these gaps.

The Rooms

Only the most vetted and cleared individuals knew of the existence and were allowed access into the inner sanctum of the British military's nerve centre in Malaya. Even the staircase leading from the main above ground buildings were camouflaged to prevent detection from the air. The Battlebox was so secret that most of the local staff at Fort Canning and many of the British officers there did not know of the inner workings of the Battlebox and what happened within its depths. Of course there were rumours about the goings-on in the bunkers. However, all staff at Fort Canning was sworn to strict secrecy and even today, several former clerks and officers who worked in the complex still refuse to talk about their experience, after keeping mum about it for more than 60 years.

Only officers and men with proper authorisation and an official need to access the Battlebox were provided with passes and the appropriate code words in order to gain entry to the underground bunkers. Code words were changed frequently and passes closely scrutinized, in order to ensure that there was no unauthorised access. As a matter of policy, the majority of officers and men allowed into the Battlebox were "White" as very few of the local "Asiatic clerks" would have been

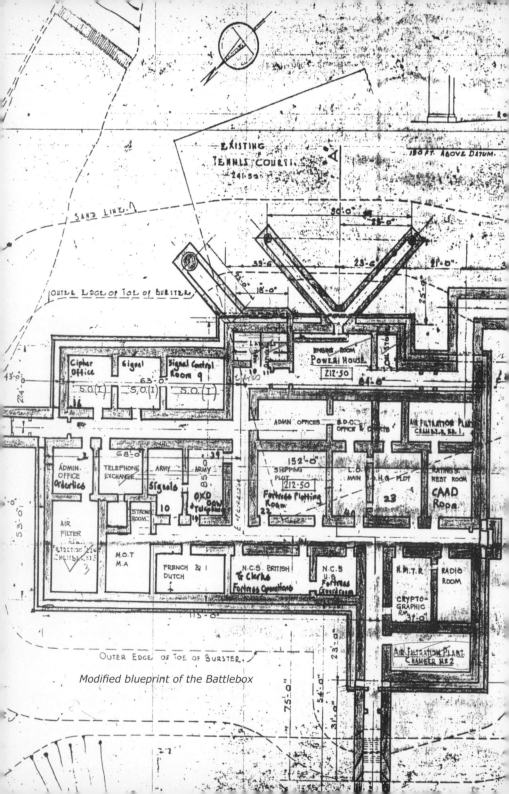

Modified blueprint of the Battlebox

trusted enough to be given access to the most sensitive secrets of Malaya Command. The only large group of non-Caucasians allowed access, were the British Indian Army sentries and guards who manned the entrances to the bunker.

Upon entering the bunker from the Cox Terrace side, one would encounter sentries almost immediately.

According to Ray Stubbs, a Royal Navy Coder who worked in the Battlebox:

> We turned down the steps to the battlebox, tunnelled into the hillside. We descended about ten steps, then up about five or six; this was apparently some kind of defence against blast and also flooding. It also provided a convenient position for the Sikh sentry to mount his guard. As our heads appeared over the peak of the barrier I could see a turbanned figure laid against the incline, rifle and bayonet straight out in front. There was a curt challenge... Once the sentry was satisfied, we passed through the concreted passageway and came eventually to our duty station.[5]

Because of the highly sensitive work being carried out in the bunkers, the Indian Army sentries were reinforced by men from the Malacca volunteers, who were also stationed at the entrances. Later, when the War reached Singapore's doorstep, most of these sentries were removed to serve at other more vital positions in defending the island.

As you came through the main solid-iron double doors, installed in case of a gas attack, there was a long hallway which was well-lit and filled with a low level buzz of the ventilation system and wall mounted lights that illuminated the chambers.

The door to each room remained locked at all times with access to each of these chambers restricted to essential personnel only. Signs stating "No Smoking", "No Eating" and "No Talking" were put up to ensure minimal disruption to operations. There were also posters warning of "loose lips" and the need for operational secrecy.

Although officers in the various rooms could communicate with one another, most rarely saw their colleagues in the other rooms. They used telephones routed through the telephone exchange and vacuum suction message tubes that lined the complex.

Using a small container wrapped in rubber, an officer would put a document in the capsule; insert it in the tube which would then be sucked to the other end of the pipe, the destination of the document. These pipes linked several key rooms like the Signal Control and Gun Operations Room as well as the XDO to the Fortress Plotting Room. Many remember the "thud" when the containers reached their destination.

Orderlies and Air Filtration Plant No 3 (Room 2)

This is where the other ranks would rest when taking breaks from their shift and also where the dispatch clerks (DLRS) would send incoming and outgoing packages and mail. This facility was eventually shifted to the signal office on the opposite side of the hallway.

A doorway inside the orderlies' room led into Air Filtration Plant No 3. Inside the Battlebox were three air filtration plants that were built to provide breathable air even during a gas attack. Because the equipment was large and generated a lot of heat, the underground complex was never very cool and when more people began to fill the corridors in the final stages of the battle for Singapore, it was absolutely boiling.

Air Filtration Plant 3. Note the size of the filtration machine and flooded interior of the room. The machine was removed and this room has now been converted into a gift shop in the Battlebox Museum.

Telephone Exchange

When the Battlebox was unsealed in 1988, the telephone exchange rooms were found with huge gaping holes in the ground, created most probably by the huge telephone exchange machines used in connecting external calls through to the various rooms in the complex and internal communications within the Battlebox.

The exchange was connected to all military and most civilian switchboards throughout Malaya as well as the military scrambler phone lines to the various units and forward positions, including most of the operational headquarters of the divisions.

As the War progressed, the signals traffic increased dramatically but the signals office in Kuala Lumpur, headquarters of Heath's III Indian Corps and the front-line headquarters for the battles raging in northern Malaya, was only connected to Fort Canning through the ordinary civilian telephone exchange.

What this meant was that it was impossible to get immediate battlefield reports and updates from northern Malaya. As the main military communications system was based on civilian phone lines, various units and divisions jammed up the available lines with urgent reports and calls for instruction, rather than relying on their antiquated and very often broken-down signals communications system. As the remaining telephone lines were also choked with civilian calls upcountry, it proved to be an untenable situation.

Routing calls through the public phone exchange meant there was a 45-minute delay even in connecting Percival to Heath in Kuala Lumpur. As quite a lot of battlefield reports and tactical discussions were conducted over the telephone system, this meant that by the time the senior officers were able to get in touch with one another, events had already overtaken the decisions that needed to be made.

Eventually, the telephone exchange at Fort Canning set up a priority list with first priority going to calls by Percival, next the scrambler phone calls to Fort Canning and then the others. With the Malayan Civil Service swamped by the onset of the war, it was impossible to get more dedicated phone lines added. It was only after Percival personally made representations to the telegraph company that it finally gave the

This photo shows what the telephone exchange looked like when it was unsealed in 1988. The hole in the floor is where the phone exchange machine was located. The present mock-up, though not the same sophisticated equipment as the original, is an example of the type of equipment used.

Signals office in Kuala Lumpur a direct line to Fort Canning. However, by this point, it proved useless as the British had lost most of northern Malaya in a matter of weeks and the war had shifted to southern Malaya. The dedicated line was used only for a week before the British evacuated Kuala Lumpur.

The Signals Section (Rooms 16, 9, unknown)

The three rooms containing the Cipher Office, Signal and Signal Control Room received most of the coded transmissions coming initially from the other two services and later from the Commander-in-Chief, Western Pacific, General Sir Archibald Wavell's office in Java. This is where outgoing messages were also sent to be transmitted to the various sub headquarters and units in the Malayan theatre and remained the only outgoing wireless circuit to London in operation, after Singapore fell.

There were two types of messages that were received, Most Important and Secret. The important messages were marked Urgent while the highly sensitive and secret messages were marked ICW, or In Cipher Wireless. This meant they were sent coded (in cipher) and paraphrased via Morse code and would require decoding on receipt before the message could be read.

Many signals from the field were sent to Fort Canning via wireless transmitting stations throughout Malaya attached to divisional head-quarters. Units were also able to raise Fort Canning using portable wireless sets and during the last days of the battle for Singapore, Fort Canning signals would receive distraught pleas for help via these wireless sets throughout the island.

All radio networks used the code and link system, which was designed to deny information to enemy intercept and intelligence services. This was done by issuing daily, secret groups of three letters (code signs) to HQs of all formations and units down to company/squadron HQs. These code signs would authenticate the signals being received and would prevent the enemy from being able to send fake messages on captured wireless equipment. The codes were changed daily at 0001 Z hours (Theatre Operations time). Sub-units merely added a figure to the code sign of the parent station and sub-sub-units a letter.[6]

Simple codes were also used to disguise map references and orders and it wasn't until 1943 that complex encoding systems like SLIDEX cards were introduced. In Malaya, pre-war codes were used but there has been no evidence so far to suggest that these early codes had been broken.

The main line of military communication on Singapore Island was through buried fixed cables which linked Fort Canning and other headquarters with all the coastal artillery sites, air strips and divisional headquarters. During the war, Command Signals was responsible for communications coming in and out of Singapore while Fortress Signals was responsible for internal communications.

Signal Room

The Signal Room was what many referred to as the 'post office'. This was where messages were picked up or sent off. It was occupied by about seven men per shift, three signal men, two orderlies and two clerks.

The shifts were arranged by Signal headquarters but the room was not locked up like most because the ventilation was very poor.[7]

A normal day would start with the signal operators receiving a situation report from the field sent via wireless or from the cables and once decoded, it would then be handed over to the signal officer, who would then forward the report to the various commands and operations rooms, and should it warrant it, finally ending up on Percival's desk.

The main types of signals received usually concerned troop movements and new dispositions on the ground. These details would be forwarded to the fortress plotting and gun operations room as well as the relevant commanders who were in need of the detailed positions.

Cipher Room

The Cipher Room was where all these messages were decoded and encoded using the various military code books and enciphering equipment. The messages sent or received were supposed to be destroyed after three days, for which a large shredder was set up.

However, when Fort Canning was bombed heavily in January 1942 and the power supply cut, the emergency generators provided an incompatible voltage for the shredder, which then had to be abandoned following which all documents had to be burned.

By late January 1942 as the Japanese advanced across southern Malaya, the cipher office was shifted out of the Battlebox and the room was left empty and non-commissioned officers began using it as a place to sleep.

Signal Control Room

The Signal Control Room was reported to have two local communication links or circuits and overseas circuits with Hong Kong, India, Ceylon and the Dutch East Indies (Indonesia), which would then relay messages to London.

Complete silence was essential in this room in order to take down the Morse code being received from the various links. A duty signal officer would be stationed here to verify and authenticate the messages received which would then be sent to the Cipher Room for decoding before being handed over for dispatch to the Signal Room. Large signal equipment lined the walls as operators with headsets manned the receiving and transmitting units. The men were divided into three shifts a day but by January 1942, it was impossible for the operators to keep up with the huge flow of traffic. More men were drafted in from signal units that had evacuated from upcountry in order to cope.

One interesting aspect of this room is the Japanese graffiti found on its walls which indicate that it was used during the Japanese Occupation. Mainly a list of Japanese soldiers and their units, one of the more curious ones is the name Percival written in Hiragana script followed by the name Yamashita (the Commander of the Japanese forces in the Malayan Campaign), underlined by the phrase, Yamashita Shogun, giving the reader no doubt as to who was the victor in this place.

The graffiti show that at least these few signal rooms were occupied by the Japanese, most probably because of their communications links and as a shelter for soldiers who were guarding the Japanese Defence Headquarters which used the external buildings during the Occupation.

Jim Howard, an Australian military photographer during the war, parachuted into Singapore on 28 August 1945, days before the official Japanese surrender, and entered the bunker complex, where he saw Japanese soldiers occupying these rooms and using the communications facilities. Obviously, the equipment was not sufficiently destroyed by the surrendering British as the Japanese were still able to use the signals equipment. Howard noted the rooms nearby were barely furnished and the Orderlies Room had bunks and were occupied by Japanese guards who also cooked there, with the stench of ammonia in the air, the result of someone using the inner recesses of the bunker as a public latrine.[8]

Original signs over the XDO Room gave the author and researchers clues as to the function of the various rooms and helped identify the room where Percival and his commanders made the decision to surrender. Parts of the XDO Room's aquamarine blue walls can be seen.

XDO, OOW & Telephones and XDO & Signals Room, (Rooms 39, 14, 10)

It is still unclear what OOW stands for but the XDO stands for the Extended Defence Office, which was a crucial element in defending the Singapore Fortress. The XDO was in command of all the local naval defence elements, including local patrol vessels as well as the navy signal stations and boom defence vessels. This was the naval liaison office with the Army, in order to better coordinate with the coastal and fixed artillery commanded by Brigadier Arthur Drury Curtis, Commander of Singapore's Fixed Defences.

Lieutenant Commander David Copley, who served as secretary to the Extended Defence Officer, described the inner workings of this almost aquamarine blue room:

> This was a medium sized room, in which were a number of wireless transmitters and receivers and benches with telephones. The walls were covered with all kinds of charts (maps of the local area), a large notice board and various of the current war time posters, warning of secrecy such as 'walls have ears'. Off this room were several doors to those parts reserved for the officer of the watch, and certainly others of a higher station. There was a slight hum from the air conditioning, supplemented by a whirring fan.

> My job there was to code and decode wireless messages, and to receive, and make telephone calls (all scrambled for security purposes). The messages by transmitter would have been to and from ships of the Royal Navy, escorting convoys in and out of Singapore, or on patrol in nearby waters. Telegraphic communication was with other military and naval establishments, such as the naval base and gunnery commands.[9]

Latrines (Rooms 10, 11)

There were latrines provided in the underground bunker, one for the use of officers and the others for non-commissioned officers and men. There were no facilities for women as the majority of bunker's personnel were male and there were no female clerks working in the Battlebox. Because they were heavily used and constantly clogging up, by the time of the Battle for Singapore in February 1942, the facilities were no longer useable and the stench from the toilets was making it hard to work in the Battlebox. Much of the toilet remains intact with the toilet bowls and urinals still standing.

At the junction in front of the latrines is a concrete pedestal. What this was used for is still unknown.

The urinals were in better condition and looked useable except that the water supply had not functioned since the early 1940s. Amazingly, the toilets were one of the few rooms that were actually dry.

Power House and Oil Store

This was the location of the emergency power generators that were to keep the Battlebox fully operational in case the power supply was cut. Vents from the engine room lead all the way to the surface on the top of the hill, where the oddly shaped mushroom structures are actually the sealed up vents. These structures still exist today and are an interesting curiosity in the park above the bunkers.

When Fort Canning became the target of heavy bombing and the external power lines were cut, these emergency generators were brought on-line to supply the electricity needed.

However, the small amount of power it generated was not enough to keep the ventilation system going at full speed so it became stiflingly hot and unbreathable in the rooms. The huge and oily concrete stumps, on which the massive generators were located, still exist today but the oil drums and most of the machinery were looted long ago. When the bunker was unsealed in 1988, the area was flooded but has since been pumped dry.

If you continue past the engine room, you come up to a passageway which turns left and then right again before it leads to a metal staircase.

The engines and electrical equipment in the power house had been stripped and all that remained was the concrete blocks and a few remnants of the machinery. It was flooded and the water was more than 5 inches deep at certain parts. There was also an oil slick from the excess oil abandoned in the bunkers. The square windows in the back were ventilation shafts. We found old t-shirts stuffed in them. An abandoned oil drum can be seen in on the left foreground.

The emergency rooftop exit was located behind the power house. The area was flooded with up to a foot of water when first opened. Today, a new rooftop structure has been installed so that visitors can get a better view of the passageway.

This was the beginnings of the emergency exit built into the underground bunker for use in escaping. The emergency exit was kept a secret from most of the bunker's inhabitants as it was only to be used by the senior commanders in case of a full scale attack on the Battlebox. Most did not know of the emergency escape hatch and staircase which remained hidden beyond the power house.

Fortress Command

Occupied by the Fortress Commander, Major General Keith Simmons, this room at present, has been recreated using one of two rare pictures of this complex obtained from the Imperial War Museum, showing how the General used it as his wartime office.

The Battlebox was actually more Simmons' headquarters than Percival's. From here, Simmons would be able to command any battle or skirmish fought on the island. Under his command, came the

Fixed Defences commanded by Curtis and the Anti Aircraft Defences, commanded by Brigadier A.W.G. Wildey.

As Percival noted in his book, *The War In Malaya*:

> The Commander of the Singapore Fortress was responsible for the defence of Singapore and adjoining islands and of the eastern area of Johore. He had under his command all the fixed defences, i.e. coast defence guns and searchlights, the anti-aircraft defences, the beach defence troops, the Straits Settlements Volunteer Force (except for the battalion at Penang), and the various fortress and administrative units. It was a pretty important command, especially as he also became heavily involved with civil problems connected with the defence of Singapore. In addition to this he had the responsibility for the defence of the east coast of Johore where the small port of Mersing, connected to Singapore by a good motor road, had always been thought to be a likely landing place for an invading force. For the defence of this area he had to rely on what field troops could be made available from Singapore — not a very satisfactory state of affairs and one about which I never felt very happy.[10]

Simmons faced an enormous challenge in commanding the final stages of the battle for Singapore. The War had already been lost and the delaying actions he was forced to take clearly took a toll. Simmons had earlier been in command of the British forces in Shanghai when he was forced to evacuate as the Japanese Army advanced. Yet again, he was faced with a similar situation. This time, Simmons refused to leave. He was interned as a POW along with Percival and the other senior commanders after the fall of Singapore. The smaller room is believed to have served as Simmons' bedroom during the last days of the campaign.

"G" Clerks Fortress Operations (Room 41)

The "G" Operations room was the main centre where field reports and dispatches would come in from the signals and various other offices and then be compiled into a situation report and submitted to Percival and his commanders. The clerks in this room were also responsible for handling all staff papers and communications for Percival and Simmons.

As part of the general staff, these men would co-ordinate all the instructions issued and distribute the various issued orders while

The "G" Clerks were responsible for dispatching and receiving all staff and administrative paper for Percival and Simmons. It was at "G" Clerks that Percival drafted his final note to British and Allied troops on the island. Note the water-logged floor.

compiling that day's summary reports and documents for the Fortress Commander. Percival's last communiqué to the troops after the surrender was issued from "G" Ops.

It was in this room, in 1988, that a decomposing stretcher was found which has now been removed. When it was used, what it was used for and what became of its occupant is still a mystery.

Fortress Plotting Room

Although details are sketchy, the rotting cork boards on the wall clearly indicate that the plotting room was filled with maps of the various areas of operations, from the initial Japanese invasion on 8 December 1941 to the last lines of defence around the burnt out town of Singapore on the morning of 15 February 1942.

The Plotting Room is believed to have been linked to the signals section and the Gun Operations room with all details of the Japanese advance and Allied troop dispositions plotted meticulously on a huge table in the centre of the room, manned by clerks and plotters who would receive decoded field movement reports on numerous telephones in the room and plot the various air and defence positions along the peninsula and finally on Singapore island itself.

This was the vertical plank, embedded in a concrete base block and discoloured and with red stains on it. Note the floor next to it has been dug up and is filled with brackish water. The wires hanging were loose pieces that were not stripped by looters. It is believed that the holes were dug by treasure hunters in the hopes of discovering hidden treasure buried in the bunker.

The room was initially built as a shipping plot to identify where the various Royal Navy elements were located and explains why it is so close to the XDO rooms. The XDO would have provided naval plotting data and intelligence would have been received to show the various positions of the enemy and Allied positions, with additional details coming from the Operations Room at the naval base.

After the first few days of the campaign, with the loss of the two capital ships, *HMS Prince of Wales* and *HMS Repulse*, the plotting room lost most of its purpose as there was no longer a need to plot the naval movements without any big ships.

It was used for the smaller evacuation operations and troop transfers but no longer served a very significant purpose until it was converted in the last few days for the battle of Singapore Island, when the combined operations headquarters moved back to Fort Canning.

It is believed that this is the room where the last naval and troop movements were plotted before the surrender.

Gun Operations Room

The Gun Operations Room is where the air attacks and details were plotted from data provided by signals and via telephone links.

The Royal Air Force's first lines of warning were highly secret radar units that provided advanced warning of Japanese air attacks over Malaya and Singapore.

Radio Detection Finding units or Radar units, and the Radar Installations and Maintenance Units based throughout Malaya and Singapore were linked by trunk lines to Filter Rooms, which would plot the various aircraft formation information, known as "tracks" and would forward it to the Fighter Operations Rooms at the various air bases and by signal circuits from Kuala Lumpur (co-ordinating all northern radar units) to the RAF Headquarters in Sime Road and to the Gun Operations Room at Fort Canning.[11]

It was in this way that the radar units spotted the first wave of Japanese bombers that were going to attack Singapore in the early hours of 8 December 1941. It was picked up by radar more than

A mock-up of the Gun Operations Room in the present museum reflects part of the original condition but with a plotting table and counters more reminiscent of the Cabinet War Rooms in London.

75 miles away from the target, which meant that it was spotted more than an hour before the actual bombings took place. Although the Filter Room had given Malaya Command and the Governor immediate warning of the Japanese air attack, it took the Governor more than 35 minutes to respond as he was unable to be located. Also, as he had given strict instructions that only he could authorise the use of the air raid sirens, the Governor's approval was crucial. In any event, though the approval was finally received, the civil authorities were still unable to locate the air raid warden responsible and so the sirens only came on after the first bombs hit Singapore at 4:15am. Although this advanced early warning system might have given the residents of Singapore precious time to prepare for the attack, the lack of appreciation for the advanced warning system meant that the initial use of radar was an exercise in futility.[12]

As the war progressed, radar units began withdrawing from upcountry and destroying their equipment before they fell into enemy hands. Most of the RDF units were withdrawn to Singapore with the various radar units linked by radio telephony sets to the Cathay Building, now a central coordinating point, from where tracks were relayed via tielines to the RAF Filter Room in Katong, which would subsequently forward the details to the Fighter Operations Room at Air Headquarters in Sime Road and to the Gun Operations Room at Fort Canning.[13]

When the forward headquarters moved back to Fort Canning on 11 February 1942, the filter room in Katong was sending the tracks directly to the Gun Operations Room at Fort Canning as contact with Air headquarters had been lost.

In the last days, the whole radar outfit was disbanded as there was nowhere left to set up radar positions and the staff of these units were offered to Malaya Command to help supplement the weary men at the Gun Operations Room.[14]

For Major Hugh Lindley-Jones, who worked in this room, it was a very trying time:

> We Gun Control Officer's job was to plot the progress of the enemy air attacks on a large table map using information received from Radar stations and visual observers, to check that the evidence was credible and then pass it on to the various anti-aircraft gun sites around the island. They were then prepared to try to shoot down the planes and knew the general direction, numbers and heights of the formations.
>
> The map on the table covered all Malaya, all the way up the Isthmus of Kra, in order to cover one of the air bases in Alor Star. The raids were plotted by little wooden markers with room for three lots of figures, the raid number, the number of planes, and the height in thousands of feet. These wooden markers showed direction and would have been three to four inches high.
>
> For this, there were at least two duty officers who were responsible that all ran smoothly and who had to intervene if they thought that anything was going astray. We also had some 10 to 15 on duty that received the information and plotted it on the map and others who relayed the news to the gun sites, generally by land telephone lines.[15]

Commander Fixed Defences

Brigadier Curtis was responsible for the fixed defences of the island. His room has also been recreated in the present museum using another rare photograph from the Imperial War Museum.

The Fixed Defences of Singapore were divided into two fire commands, i.e. the Changi Fire Command which covered the approaches to the Naval Base and the Faber Fire Command which covered the approaches to Keppel Harbour and the western channel of the Johore Straits. Each Fire Command had one 15-inch gun, one 9.2 inch gun and a number of 6-inch guns as well as searchlights and other equipment.

Brigadier Curtis' role was to make use of the Fortress Plotting and Gun Operations Room to ensure that accurate information was being relayed to the coastal artillery and additional fixed positions on the island to ensure that any intruders from the sea were destroyed.

Even before the enemy launched its assault from the Skudai and Melayu rivers on the opposite bank of Singapore island on the night of 7 February 1942, Curtis had already ordered the big guns on the island to traverse round and provide supporting and harassing fire on the Johore

A mock-up of the Commander Fixed Defences Room, showing Brigadier A.C. Curtis at his desk. The mock-up is based on a rare photograph taken within the bunker complex.

Straits. It was a myth that the guns of Singapore could not be traversed 180 degrees and the heavy fire on the northwestern shores during the battle for Singapore clearly proves this.

However, of greater significance was the fact that these guns, which were meant to fire on ships, were armed with mainly armour piercing (AP) shells. AP shells had only a small charge in its head which would explode upon hitting the ship's hull causing much damage.

On land, however, most of the shells would hit the ground with a loud thud and not cause much damage. As the guns were meant to target ships, there were very few High Explosive or HE shells in their magazines. The HE shells which were needed to cause significant damage to troops and armour was in very short supply. So, while the guns were able to provide artillery support, they proved ineffective because of the wrong type of ammunition (see table opposite).

Lieutenant-Colonel C.C.M. Macleod-Carey, who was at the Faber Fire Command, recounts the communication with the Fixed Defence HQ at the Fort Canning Battlebox in those last few days [16]:

> It was Friday, 13 February 1942 and I was watching the sun rise from my command post on top of Mount Faber, Singapore. The rays from the red orb of the sun radiated in ever widening shafts of red; just like the old 'Rising Sun' flag of Japan used to be.
>
> I remember that I was feeling pretty gloomy at the time but this evil omen gave me an uncomfortable sense of impending doom. Singapore at that time was obviously in its death throes and there seemed very little future in it...
>
> ...About midnight the following night, a signal came from HQ at Fort Canning saying an unidentified ship had been located just outside the minefield covering the entrances to Keppel Harbour and that no British ship was in the area. I was at that time second in command of the 7th Coast Artillery Regiment covering Keppel Harbour with its powerful armament of 15-in, 9.2 in, 6-in and a host of other smaller weapons. There was another similarly equipped regiment defending the Naval Base at Changi. I rang up the port War Signal Station, our line with the Navy, which was manned by sailors. There was no reply and we discovered later that it had been evacuated but for some reason no one had informed us. I then ordered the 6-in batteries at Serapong, Siloso and Labrador to sweep the area

TABLE OF AMMUNITION [16]

Commander Fixed Defences   **Brig. A. D. Curtiss**
7th Coast Artillery Regiment   **Faber Fire Command**

	Guns	Max Range (yards)		Ammunition (rpg)
Buona Vista Bty	2 x 15in	36,900	250AP	no HE
Connaught Bty	3 x 9.2in	31,600	250AP	30 HE
Pasir Laba Bty	2 x 6in	17,000	500AP	50 HE
Siloso Bty	2 x 6in	17,000	500AP	50 HE
Labrador Bty	2 x 6in	17,000	500AP	50 HE
Serapong Bty	2 x 6in	17,000	500AP	50 HE
Silingsing Bty	2 x 6in	17,000	500AP	50 HE

9th Coast Artillery Regiment   **Changi Fire Command**

	Guns	Max Range (yards)		Ammunition (rpg)
Johore Bty	3 x 15in	36,900	250AP	no HE
Tekong Bty	3 x 9.2in	31,600	250AP	30 HE
Sphinx Bty	2 x 6in	21,700	600AP	50 HE
Pengerang Bty	2 x 6in	21,700	600AP	50 HE
Beting Kusah Bty	2 x 6in	21,700	600AP	50 HE
Changi Bty	2 x 6in	21,700	600AP	50 HE

15in and 9.2in guns were manned by British gunners. All 6in guns were manned by Hong Kong and Singapore gunners, all Punjabis from India. There were also 11 minor associated batteries with a total of seven 12pdr and 20pdr quick-firers.

with their searchlights. Almost immediately a ship which seemed to be of 8,000 tons was illuminated at a range of 7,000 yards just outside the minefield. We challenged the ship by Aldis lamp but the reply, also by lamp, was incorrect.

Fortunately, in order to assist in this sort of situation, the Navy had posted an excellent rating who was standing by my side. We had a copy of 'Jane's Fighting Ships' and the rating pointed to a photograph of a Japanese landing craft carrier and said, 'I reckon that's it, sir'. I gave the order to 'shoot' and within seconds all 6-in guns opened up with a roar. The guns had been permanently sited and even without radar, which had not been installed, their instruments and range finding gear were so accurate that preliminary ranging was unnecessary. Direct hits were scored at once. Flames, sparks and debris started flying in all directions. The crew could be seen frantically trying to lower boats but it was all over in a matter of minutes, after which the ship just disappeared to sea.

This action was reported to Fort Canning but it is strange that it has never, so far as I know, been mentioned in an official account. Most likely the record was lost together with a good many other documents in the subsequent events after the surrender of Singapore.

Next morning, we were ordered to fire the guns at the very large number of oil tanks situated on the islands around Pulau Bukum about three miles from Keppel. Something like 200,000 tons of oil were set on fire.

Commander Anti-Aircraft Defence Room (Room 27)

Of all the rooms, this would probably be the one of greatest historical significance as it was in this room that the decision to surrender Singapore to the Japanese was taken on the morning of 15 February 1942.

The CAAD Room was initially occupied by Brigadier Wildey of the Royal Artillery.

As Percival noted, Wildey was responsible for the defence of selected targets in the Singapore area against hostile air attack. He had under his command four heavy anti-aircraft regiments, one light anti-aircraft regiment less one battery which was under the III Indian Corps, and one searchlight regiment. During an attack, Percival noted that the RAF's Group Captain Rice, the coordinator of the air defence of the Singapore area, was authorised to issue orders to him direct. Most of the guns were static and the range of the 3.7's was "very limited by modern standards" [17].

While in captivity, Wildey along with several other senior officers prepared reports of their various commands and in the documents now with the Imperial War Museum, he outlined the preparation for the anti-aircraft defence[18]:

> In the three years before Dec 1941, the A.A. defences had been fortunate in having had excellent co-operation by the R.A.F. not only in day-to-day routine flying, but in connection with some fifteen combined exercises spread over this period each lasting three days. These exercises were in the nature of "Silent Practice" for both guns and aircraft and results in every case were closely analysed and compared with those previous exercises. They were of the utmost value in training of Gun Control Room (Gun Operations

A mock-up of what the CAAD Room looked like on 15 February 1942, as Percival and his senior commanders met in the room to decide the fate of 100,000 British and Commonwealth troops in Malaya. Although the large oil tank occupied a quarter of the room, it has now been removed in order to accommodate audio visual equipment.

Room in Fort Canning), Fighter Control Room, Observer Units and Bty. Command Posts, and in developing a sound technique.

...Static gun positions for the defences of Singapore had been developed in accordance with the W.O. (War Office) plan of 1936, as amended and extended by the plan approved by the C. of S. (Chiefs of Staff) Sub-committee in 1940. Construction of new positions was proceeding with the estimated dates of arrival of new equipments and of recruits, on arrival of new units. It was up to date, though far from complete, in Dec. 1941...

...Communications between Gun Control Room and such positions as had been completed were functioning fully, and communication between the G.C.R. and Fighter Operations Room was entirely satisfactory. In addition, an observer tower, manned by a special team of observers and look out men had been established in the Naval Base, to give warning of the approach of low flying attacks on installations in the Naval Base. This tower was connected tele-phonically to Bofors troop and gun stations, G.C.R., and Naval Operations and A.R.P. (Air Raid Precaution) HQs. A function of the tower, which had a very wide range of visibility, was to provide the Gun Control Officer with a running commentary on the progress of enemy raids...

... The total number of hostile aircraft destroyed during the campaign was 130, verified by independent observation. This figure is up to approximately 8 Feb., after which no accurate returns could be obtained, though a number are known to have shot down after that date. Including them and probables it is safe to say that some 200 Japanese aircraft were put out of action permanently by A. A. D.

Although the report outlines the actions taken by the anti-aircraft units with direction from Fort Canning, Wildey, however, was upset over the lack of mobility among his troops and more importantly, effective control of the defences:

... the static equipment were at a great disadvantage compared with the mobile ones, especially after the Japanese had reached the North Shore of the JOHORE STRAITS. For lack of transporters and transport, guns had to be abandoned as the enemy advanced into the island.

... The second lesson is this: that in a fortress such as Singapore an air defence commander(as distinct from an A.A. Defence Commander) should be appointed. Only when all the means of air defence, including fighter aircraft are under one commander, can the best air defence be achieved. The appointment of an A.D. Commander was repeatedly pressed in the month before December 1941, but the only concession was the appointment of an Air Defence Co-ordinator, who had no command over available fighter aircraft, and who functioned largely through an Air Defence Committee, whose recommendation had first to be notified by the chiefs of the three services before they became operative. A very great deal of useful work was done by this committee, and during operations the liaison between the A.A.D. Commander and the co-ordinator and their staff was always cordial and satisfactory, but it is certain that had there been a Commander, Air defence, with fighter aircraft actually under his command, a better air defence of Singapore could have been achieved with the means available.[19]

Brigadier Wildey's report summed up the air defence situation in the closing days of the battle. Once the RAF had pulled out its remaining aircraft, by the middle of January 1942, the anti-aircraft guns were no longer needed to defend the air fields and aerodromes, thus many were disbanded to form infantry units. This meant the skies over Singapore were clear for Japanese aircraft to bomb the town at will, with Fort Canning receiving a major brunt of the bombing and artillery shelling.[20]

The situation got so bad that the above ground buildings were continually being hit and smouldering fires could be seen all over the hill command. It was because of the impunity with which the Japanese were bombing the British command that Percival decided to hold his final conference in the bomb-proof Battlebox.

It is curious that when the Battlebox was opened in 1988, a huge rectangular tank was found occupying much of this room. It was later discovered to be an oil storage tank and pipes in the room suggested it was used as a supply for the diesel generators which powered the ventilation system in the complex.

As more than a third of the small room was occupied by the tank, there was obviously a very limited amount of space. Moreover, the noise and smell from the tank would have made it impossible to work in for any prolonged period of time.

Although it was Wildey's room, it is believed that he would have barely used it in the lead up to and then the final battle for Singapore. As such it must have been one of the only vacant rooms in the bunker and one of the closest rooms to the Gun Operations and Plotting Room where details were coming in on the last movements of troops and air defences before the final surrender. It must have been very uncomfortable for close to ten persons to squeeze into the CAAD Room and even harder to concentrate given the unbreathable air and stiflingly hot conditions in the bunker. Nonetheless, this is where the final decision was taken to surrender Singapore.

Although the role of each room in the underground complex has been explained, there is still much to be said on how the Battlebox came to be the final location set for the decision of the final surrender, especially since Percival had moved his headquarters to Sime Road just two days before the Japanese invasion on Malaya.

What now unfolds is the story of the relocation of Malaya Command's nerve centre and how, despite the creation of a new combined headquarters, it finally ended up in a retreat to the Battlebox in less than two months.

Endnotes

1   Firbank, L.T. *A History of Fort Canning*. unpublished typescript, Singapore, c.1960s. p. 2.

2   Ibid, p. 3.

3   Ibid, p. 8.

4   Percival, A.E. *The War in Malaya*. Eyre & Spottiswoode, London, 1949.

5   *Stubbs, Ray, Personal Account, The Battlebox : Research Clippings* (date unknown), Oral History Department, Singapore.

6   Forty, George. *British Army Handbook 1939-1945*. Sutton Publishing, Gloucestershire, 1998. p. 90.

7   *The Battlebox : Research Clippings* (date unknown), Oral History Department, Singapore.

8   *Howard, Jim, Personal Account, The Battlebox : Research Clippings* (date unknown), Oral History Department, Singapore.

9   *Copley, David. Personal Account, The Battlebox : Research Clippings* (date unknown), Oral History Department, Singapore.

10 Percival, A.E. *The War in Malaya*. Eyre & Spottiswoode, London, 1949. p. 49-50.

11 *History of the RDF organisation in the Far East 1941-2, Papers of Wing Commander T.C. Carter P180.* The Imperial War Museum, London.

12 Ibid, p.5.

13 Ibid, p. 6.

14 Ibid, p.10.

15 *Lindley-Jones, Hugh. Personal Account, The Battlebox : Research Clippings*, Oral History Department, Singapore.

16 Macleod-Carey,CCM. *Singapore Guns, War Monthly*, Issue 34, p.34-39.

17 Percival, A.E. *The War in Malaya*. Eyre & Spottiswoode, London, 1949.

18 *Report on A.A. Defences Malaya, Dec.1941–Feb 1942, Papers of A.E. Percival*, P16-27. The Imperial War Museum, London, p. 4.

19 Ibid p. 5.

20 *Papers of Brigadier AWG Wildey, 98/16/1.* The Imperial War Museum, London.

Chapter 4

The Battlebox and the Combined Operations Headquarters

Although the Battlebox remained a crucial piece in the command and control of Malaya Command, it was, by 1941, too small to house all the operational staff Percival required for a unified headquarters:

> In order to ensure co-operation in war a bomb-proof battle head-quarters was constructed at Fort Canning, where it was intended that the Combined Operations Staff of the three services should work. This headquarters, however, was already too small by the time it was completed and, although it was occupied during the operations, it was never actually used for the purpose intended.[1]

Despite this, the Battlebox played a crucial role as a result of the lack of a real combined operations headquarters but more on this later.

Percival, who had taken over as General Officer Commanding, Malaya Command in July 1941, decided to create a new Combined Operations Headquarters in Singapore.

He was now tasked to prepare Malaya for a possible attack by Japan and was under enormous pressure to ensure the three services were working towards this. Percival became very good friends with the RAF's Air Officer Commanding, Air Vice-Marshal C.W.H. Pulford:

> There was some consolation, however, and that was in the person of the Air Officer Commanding Far East, Air Vice-Marshall C.W.H. Pulford, who had a short time before arrived to take over command. An ex-naval officer and a keen exponent of the torpedo-bomber

in naval warfare, he was a man of my own way of thinking in most matters military or non-military. We immediately struck up a close friendship which was to endure until we parted on the eve of the fall of Singapore, he to meet his death with the rear-admiral (Admiral Spooner) and I to spend long years in captivity. As my family was not with me, he lived with me at Flagstaff House, and I believe that our close comradeship was not an unimportant factor in fostering the spirit of co-operation which, from the time of our arrival, developed between our respective Services both on the headquarters staffs and in the field units.[2]

Flagstaff House was located on Sime Road, a huge double-storey bungalow, just before the Singapore Golf Club, sharing the same road.

Percival's home was just next door to the brand new RAF headquarters, which had been completed in 1940. The RAF had been looking for a suitable headquarters for several years and numerous locations at Oxley Rise and Institution Hill had been considered before the Air Ministry agreed to the large site on Sime Road. The Headquarters would also be home to the Air Officer Commanding and provide administrative and operations rooms for the RAF. Initial costs for the new headquarters rose to £218,700 and were eventually approved with construction completed in two years.[3]

Air Vice Marshal C.W.H. Pulford,
Air Officer Commanding, RAF Malaya

As the AOC's residence was enormous and RAF Headquarters was already short of space, Pulford decided to move in with Percival while his residence was then used as part of the headquarters office space.

As Pulford was one of the few who actually supported Percival in the internal politics of Malaya Command, it seemed logical for Percival to co-locate his new combined operations headquarters with the RAF, which would not only be next door to his residence but he would also be able to count on the support and help from his friend who would be working just next door.

However, the other Chiefs in Singapore did not feel the need to re-locate. As a result, the navy only provided liaison officers at the combined headquarters but decisions could never be made by these low-level representatives:

> In 1936 the headquarters of the Naval Commander were in Singapore City. The Army headquarters were at Fort Canning, also in Singapore City, but those of the Royal Air Force were at Seletar on the north side of the island. In order to improve cooperation, the then AOC moved his headquarters into Singapore City, but about the same time the Naval headquarters were moved to the Naval Base on the north side of the island, to enable the commander to supervise better the rapid developments which were taking place there...

> ... When the Commander-in-Chief, Far East (Air Chief Marshal Sir Robert Brooke-Popham) was appointed (1941), the problem of the location of headquarters again came to the front. If his headquarters had been located in the Singapore city area they would have been closer to those of the Army and Air Force and of the Civil Government, but would have been separated from those of the Commander-in-Chief China Station with whom much preliminary planning had to be done. Also the Far East Combined Bureau (Intelligence) which had come under the Commander-in-Chief China Station was located at the Naval Base. The Commander-In-Chief Far East was largely dependent on this bureau for his intelligence. He therefore decided to establish his headquarters at the Naval Base with the intention of moving to the Sime Road area should operations develop in Malaya. This is what actually happened.[4]

Brooke-Popham gave Percival immediate permission to build the new combined operations headquarters at Sime Road and work began without prior funding allocated from Whitehall. This upset the administrative mandarins at the War Office and Air Ministry as no funding approval or tender had been sought for the building of the new headquarters.

The Chief Engineer, Far East, had appointed the construction firm of Tan Eng Wah (the lowest of seven bids) in August 1940 to build the RAF's hutted office accommodation. Later, temporary accommodation was needed and Tan Eng Wah was paid a further £20,000 to carry it out. However, by mid 1941, there was no time left to call for quotes and tenders so the Chief Engineer gave the £120,000 Combined headquarters project to Tan Eng Wah. After strong objection, Whitehall finally gave approval for a waiver of tender for the project on 17 January 1942, a month after the complex had already been built and three weeks before the Sime Road headquarters was abandoned to the advancing Japanese. However, it is not clear whether Tan Eng Wah was ever paid the full £120,000 as Singapore fell very shortly after the headquarters was completed.[5]

The new requirements for the combined headquarters were big. Office accommodation was built for 100 officers, 230 other ranks and 35 "Asiatic clerks", and housing for 42 officers, 5 warrant officers, 50 sergeants, 150 other ranks and 25 clerks, comprising, "hutted accommodation for officers, officers mess and single officers' quarters, sergeants mess and quarters, huts for rank and file with dining halls, cookhouses, institutes, bath houses and latrines, large combined operations room, signal offices, guard room, mechanical and electrical services and all external services, with camouflage". The buildings would be dispersed in a rubber plantation and this would involve the extension of roads, lighting, water and drainage.[6]

By September 1941, the War Office informed Malaya Command that the Treasury's Inter-Service Committee had finally agreed to spend the £120,000, as an "operational necessity" [7] for "the extension of the accommodation to house, in temporary construction, the headquarters of the Army Command, Malaya, together with some additional Royal Air Force personnel, and to the erection of a combined operations room..." [8]

The new facilities at Sime Road consisted of several rows of hutted offices. On one side was RAF headquarters and on the other Army headquarters. The GOC and AOC, as well as senior officers, had offices located about a hundred yards from the Combined Operations Room.

Adjoining these offices, was the Combined Operations Room, where the staff officers and clerks of the two services could work and plot the progress of operations. The room was filled with large plotting tables, charts and manned round the clock. The room had direct phone lines to the Battlebox and the war room at the Naval Base, as well as secure links to the III Indian Corps in Kuala Lumpur, via the telephone exchange at Fort Canning. The RAF had also built an independent wireless transmitting station at Sime Road and this would be used for all signals traffic generated by the Combined Headquarters.

The Battlebox at Fort Canning, however, would still remain crucial in operations. The Anti-Aircraft Gun Operations Room, which plotted air movements and was in control of all AA positions (which were mainly near airbases) in Malaya, was still located at the underground communications centre. The Naval Extended Defence Office, which controlled the sea-lanes off Singapore, would also remain at the Battlebox. Simmons, the Fortress Commander, took charge of the Battlebox, in order to coordinate the defence of Singapore.

On 6 December, 1941, barely two days before the Japanese invasion, the new combined headquarters at Sime Road was finally completed.

> ...It will thus be seen when hostilities started the headquarters of the Army, the Royal Air Force and of the Civil Government were grouped in one area (Sime Road and Government House), while those of the Commanders-In-Chief and of the Rear-Admiral Malaya were grouped in another (Naval Base), some 10 miles or more apart. This was far from an ideal solution, but possibly the best under the circumstances... This problem of the location of headquarters has been discussed at some length as showing the difficulties of reconciling the requirements of independent Services. Had there at that time been a Supreme Commander with an integrated staff probably many of these difficulties would have disappeared... The location of headquarters of the two Commanders-in-Chief and of the Fighting Services was a problem which received a great amount of attention but which was never satisfactorily settled. Probably there was no satisfactory solution.[9]

The new headquarters would prove to be a real challenge due to the poor construction of the buildings, the lack of space and the fact that most of the time the entire staff and commanders of the two headquarters would be in the combined operations room as their offices were too far away from the room.

However, even before the war started, Headquarters Malaya Command was faced with a more pressing problem — manpower:

... With the increase in the garrison as the defences developed and the relations with Japan became more strained, so there was an increase in the strength of Headquarters Malaya Command. The senior General Staff Officer, who had been a 2nd Grade Staff Officer in 1935, became a Brigadier in 1940. The senior Administrative Staff Officer was a Brigadier i/c Administration who, as is customary, was responsible to the War Office for control of expenditure on the administrative side. With the expansion of the command in 1941, the "A" and "Q" Branches were separated, a Deputy Adjutant General being appointed as Head of the "A" Branch while the Brigadier i/c Administration remained responsible for the "Q" Branch...

... After the outbreak of war with Germany the filling of vacancies on the staff became more and more difficult as the supply of trained staff officers in the Far East became exhausted. Regular units serving in Malaya were called upon to supply officers with qualifications until it became dangerous to weaken them any further and selected officers were sent for a short course of training at Quetta. The supply of trained officers from Home was naturally limited by the non-availability and by the difficulties of transportation...

... In 1941, sea voyages from the United Kingdom were taking 2 to 3 months so that there was a long delay in filling staff vacancies from Home even after approval had been given. In consequence, the strength of Headquarters Malaya Command was usually much below establishment. When war with Japan broke out there were less than 70 officers on Headquarters Malaya Command, including the Headquarters of the Services. This is about the war-time establishment of the Headquarters of a Corps. Our resources were thus strained to the limit...

... At the same time even before war broke out with Japan, the work at Headquarters Malaya Command was particularly heavy, including as it did war plans and the preparation of a country for war in addition to the training and administration of a rapidly increasing garrison. In addition, the Command was responsible for placing orders to bring up to the approved scale the reserves of all supplies and stores except as regards weapons and ammunition. In fact, Headquarters Malaya Command combined the functions of a local War Office and those of a Headquarters of a Field Force. [10]

Despite these challenges, the Combined Operations Room and the new headquarters at Sime Road were up and running on the morning of 6th December 1941. However, Percival would not be there to inaugurate the opening of the new complex. He was in Kuala Lumpur meeting with Brooke-Popham and Heath, discussing whether to implement Operation MATADOR, an offensive plan to capture parts of Siam (Thailand) and prevent a Japanese bridgehead, based on reports that Japanese troops would shortly be landing in Malaya.

The Location

There has been much controversy in recent years as to the location of the Combined Operations Headquarters at Sime Road.

A plaque was set up by the National Heritage Board next to a pill box on Sime Road to mark the site and it reads as follows, "The gun shelter, built sometime before 1941, defended Flagstaff House, the operational Headquarters of the British Army and Air Force during the Malayan Campaign".

Many have criticised the authorities for putting up the plaque firstly because they say Flagstaff House was never in Sime Road and as such the pill box could not have been built some time before 1941 to defend the Combined Headquarters which was only set up in early December 1941.

The criticisms have been leveled because the history and location of the Combined Operations Headquarters were shrouded in secrecy in 1941 and with most of its occupants dead during the war; a proper account of its use has never been given.

The mystery still continues to haunt researchers as a majority of documents relating to the combined headquarters were destroyed in the fall of Singapore.

However, recently declassified files at the National Archives in London have provided a map of the area where the Combined Operations

Headquarters was located, which shows the above ground buildings that were constructed from the late 1930s to 1941.

There are two maps, which were declassified in the early 1970s and show the Sime Road area.

The first is a blueprint showing the layout of RAF Headquarters Far East in Sime Road in 1939, before the decision to set up a combined headquarters and combined operations room. It shows clearly a huge compound that was built by the RAF to house its headquarters, when it was shifted from Seletar by Pulford.

The new compound, with the AOC's house, was next to Flagstaff House, Percival's official residence, on Sime Road. On the blueprint, Flagstaff House is not listed but the building has been drawn in. As it is adjacent to the AOC's House, the residence next door was clearly Flagstaff House.

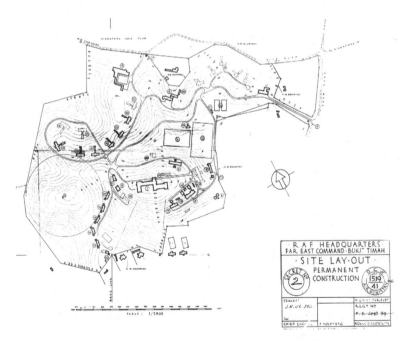

Blueprint from 1939 showing the layout of
RAF Headquarters Far East in Sime Road.

Therefore, the pill box located on Sime Road, was built to guard the RAF Headquarters and the AOC's Residence, work on which had begun in 1939. Flagstaff House and the RAF Headquaters and can be seen on the map but Flagstaff House was never the operational headquarters of the Army and Air Force. The AOC's house, however, was used as offices by RAF Headquarters. Therefore, the pill box did end up being used to guard Flagstaff House, the AOC's residence and the combined operations headquarters.

The newer map, an extracted photocopy of a larger map dating from the early 1950s, shows the two houses but the AOC's residence had changed in shape and structure and was now labeled, Commander-in-Chief's Residence (C-in-C, Far East Air Force), while the pre-war GOC's residence (Flagstaff House) was labeled as private property.

The post-war map also showed the hutted structures built in 1941 to accommodate the new army headquarters and the combined operations room. The long lines of hutted offices on the map were part of where the Army and RAF headquarters were located.

The 1950s map also shows a plotting shed in the Commander-in-Chief's compound and ancillary facilities that are labeled as part of the HQ Malaya area. The RAF Headquarters was shifted to Changi and renamed HQ FEAF (HQ Far East Air Force). The offices in Sime Road were taken over by the Air Ministry's Department of General Works (AMDGW) as well as by the MPBW HQ (Ministry of Public Buildings and Works). As there was obviously no need for a plotting shed for the works departments, the shed and the office buildings nearby must have been part of the earlier Combined Operations Headquarters. Just opposite the AMDGW offices are the outlines of a building, which are believed to be some of the hutted offices of the Army. Together, this whole area would have been the nerve centre of the British and Commonwealth land and air forces as the Malayan Campaign began.

Many of the bungalows and residences listed in the 1939 blueprint do not exist on the 1950s map as many were not built due to financial constraints while other structures were added as part of the new complex. The RAF Headquarters building as listed in the 1939 blueprint also does not exist, giving more support to the fact that the AOC's residence was used as offices for RAF Headquarters.

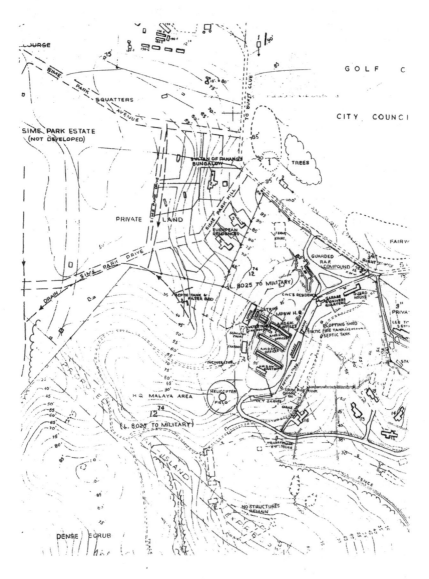

Post World War II map from the 1950s showing the layout
of military buildings at the Sime Road Complex.

The map of the post-war RAF compound, shows the residence of the Far East Air Force's Commander-in-Chief, which had come to be known as Air House or the Air Marshal's House. Admiralty records from the post-war period show that the Air Officer Commanding, RAF, no longer shared accommodation with the GOC at Flagstaff House but now resided at Cluny Road. The Commander-in-Chief, Far East Land Forces, who was based in Singapore, now took over Flagstaff House while the General Officer Commanding, Malaya Command (and subsequently Singapore Base District), moved into Draycott House along Stevens Road.[11]

Another residence on Kheam Hock Road, Command House, was temporarily occupied by the GOC before he moved to Draycott House and Command House then became the residence of the Chief Justice.

In Colonial Office correspondence from the late 1950s, Command House, Air House and Flagstaff House were named as choices for the new residence of the UK Commissioner-General for Southeast Asia.[12] With Yusof Ishak appointed as the Yang Di-Pertuan Negara (Head of State) of Singapore, there was no longer a British Governor of Singapore and the Commissioner General, Lord Selkirk, based in Singapore, would then be the most senior UK representative on the island and would have to have a residence befitting that stature. The Commissioner General eventually became the British High Commissioner to Singapore when the Republic gained independence in 1965. In the end, the Colonial Office decided not to take any of the three options but rather to keep Eden Hall, the earlier residence of the Commissioner General.

Command, Air and Flagstaff House were handed over to the Singapore Government sometime in 1971 as part of the disposal of British military real estate, when the British forces finally pulled out of the island. Treasury minutes valued Flagstaff House at £414,650, Air House and the surrounding land at £1,025,521 and Command House at £239,312. The files, declassified in 2004, indicate that the Singapore Government received these residences and numerous other military facilities and moveable assets as gifts worth about £135 million (S$405 Million) when the British pulled out.[13] This was in addition to the £50 Million committed by the British Government in 1968, over a five-year period, to mitigate the economic effects of the planned withdrawal of British forces in the area. However, the £135 million figure was revised down to £109 million as the British government decided to hold on to the MPBW HQ and the compound surrounding Air House at Sime Road as well as several other facilities in Singapore for a while longer. Most of these facilities are believed to have been eventually handed over to the Singapore Government.[14]

Command House was then occupied by independent Singapore's first Chief Justice and later became the official residence of the Speaker of Parliament but remained unused by him. It was then refurbished in the 1990s and used temporarily as the residence of the President of Singapore while the Istana (Government House) was being restored.

At present Command House lies vacant. There is no information on what happened to Air House and Flagstaff House, or who are their present occupants, after the buildings were handed back to the Singapore government. Today, the combined headquarters area at Sime Road has been redeveloped but some of the bungalows attached to the compound have been preserved and are at present being rented out to expatriates who enjoy living in one of the few "black and white" colonial homes on the island.

Endnotes

1   Percival, A.E. *The War in Malaya*. Eyre & Spottiswoode, London, 1949.

2   Ibid

3   *0.5., Command Headquarters, 26 October 1938, Air Ministry File No: S35559/Pt II, AIR2/1603*. The National Archives, London.

4   Percival, A.E. *The War in Malaya*. Eyre & Spottiswoode, London, 1949.

5   *275, D.U.S.,15 January, 1942, Air Ministry File No: S35559/Pt II, AIR2/1603*. The National Archives, London.

6   *Accomodation for Army Headquarters, Malaya, at Bukit Timah, Treasury Inter-Service Committee, August, 1941, AIR2/1603*. The National Archives, London

7   Ibid

8   *118/MALAYA/207(F.W.1b), 29 September, 1941, AIR2/1603*. The National Archives, London.

9   *Percival, A.E. Draft of Despatches, P16-27.* The Imperial War Museum, London.

10 Ibid

11 *Land Occupied by the United Kingdom Services in Singapore, undated, ADM1/28453.* The National Archives, London.

12 *Extract from note about accommodation for the U.K. Commission in Singapore, c1959, CO1030/873.* The National Archives, London.

13 *Undated Treasury Minute, 1971 concerning the gift of fixed assets and equipment to the Government of Malaysia (Singapore portion), WO32/21583.* The National Archives, London.

14 *Undated Treasury Minute, 1971 concerning the gift of fixed assets and equipment to the Government of Singapore, WO32/21684.* The National Archives, London.

Chapter 5

The Battlebox and the
Malayan Campaign

As the battle for Malaya began on 8 December 1941 and the losses on
the British side began to mount, the mood in the Combined Operations
headquarters became sombre indeed. As state after Malayan state fell
to the oncoming Japanese while the Allies retreated, there was a sense
of gloom in Sime Road that the end was nearing.

> The new combined headquarters for the army and RAF had only
> opened in Sime Road just two days before hostilities began.
> Although the main operations and war room were now located
> at the combined headquarters, the Navy still operated its own
> operations room at the Naval Base and stationed liaison officers
> at the Sime Road headquarters. Moreover, the Battlebox at Fort
> Canning would still be occupied by Simmons, along with the anti-
> aircraft Gun Operations Room and the Naval extended defences
> offices. This meant that the battle for Malaya would be fought from
> the new Sime Road headquarters while the Singapore defences
> and operations would be carried out of the Battlebox, with the
> exception of anti-aircraft gun defences for Malaya which would still
> be run out of the Battlebox.[1]

In theory, there was a very clear separation of duties and lines of
communication. In practice, however, the lack of skilled manpower to
run two almost identical war rooms and insufficient clarity among field
commanders and officers in Malaya meant that many operational calls

and signals were still being routed to Fort Canning which then had to be re-routed to Sime Road. As a result, the decentralised war rooms created greater confusion and down time as it took ages for ground intelligence and reports to filter up and be represented on duplicate situation charts and plots so that planners at Sime Road could work on an attack strategy while plotters at the Battlebox could advise anti-aircraft batteries throughout the peninsula to open fire on targets.

Headquarters Malaya Command took its signals situation seriously. Command Signals was responsible for communication sent outside the island while Fortress Signals was responsible for signals within the island. However, this distinction became blurred with the quick losses faced up-country and Fortress Signals ended up with the role of keeping the battlebox and combined headquarters operational. It was critical that the command headquarters and formations remain in communication and Fortress Signals worked continuously in the days leading up to hostilities, preparing the various trunk and cable lines for use by field and rear headquarters.

On the first of December, Fortress Signal's War Diary showed that at 1100hrs, the codeword "SEAVIEW" had been issued, the command for troops to move forward into prepared positions throughout Malaya. An hour later, the codeword "OILCAN" was issued, ordering the mobilisation of the Federated Malay States Volunteer Force.[2]

By 6 December 1941, it was clear that the Japanese were going to attack and after meetings with Heath in Kuala Lumpur, Brooke-Popham, in consultation with Percival, ordered Fortress Signals to issue the codeword "RAFFLES", the order to bring all troops to the first degree of readiness.[3]

The amount of intelligence predicting a Japanese attack was overwhelming. Air reconnaissance and intercepted signals traffic had indicated an impending Japanese fleet headed towards Malaya. Prior to the outbreak of War, signals intelligence became crucial in determining the state of readiness of the Japanese forces and their exact plans in attacking Malaya.

A "Y" SIGINT (Signal Intelligence) Unit had been set up at the RAF wireless transmitting station in Kranji (No. 52 W.U.), picking up information on the strengths of the Japanese naval air arm from air to ground and ground to air traffic. [4]

The "Y" unit was part of the Far East Combined Bureau, set up in Hong Kong in 1934 and charged with the interception and decoding of Japanese signal intelligence. The FECB was officially known as the Centre for Operational Intelligence and Signals (COIS), which provided the most sensitive and secret operational information for British commanders in the field.

The FECB was based at the headquarters of and reported to the Commander-in-Chief, China Fleet, Vice Admiral Sir Geoffrey Layton at the Naval Base in northern Singapore. As this was a major source of intelligence, Brooke-Popham also needed to be close to this facility and so did not locate himself at the Battlebox at Fort Canning or in the Combined Headquarters at Sime Road. What this meant was that the Commander-in-Chief, Far East and the Naval Commander for Malaya were based at the Naval Base while the Army and Air Commanders were based at Sime Road. Thus the defences of Malaya were split between the Naval Base and Sime Road, with the Battlebox becoming a third command centre to take charge of the Singapore aspect of operations.

As a result, all intelligence information received and decoded had to be routed by the FECB to the two other service chiefs at Sime Road with a copy to the Battlebox as needed:

> In Hong Kong days the office of the Captain of the Staff China Station, in practice, formed the intelligence Section of the Sigint Organisation which predominated over it in numbers but was itself administratively under the COIS. At Hong Kong and later Singapore where it was known as the FECB, the COIS organisation was an inter-service one and equipped to handle collation and dissemination of Naval, Military, Air and Political Intelligence. [5]

The dissemination of intelligence was sent by 'Most Secret' signals originated by FECB. In their offices at the naval base and Fort Canning, a card index of naval and naval air intelligence was started and although some reference to back material was possible, a lack of manpower meant that there was no production of regular summaries.

Although the FECB suffered from insufficient manpower, the receiving stations picked up very useful intelligence that was becoming more worrisome by the day. Signs of Japanese intentions for an attack were obvious in the intercepted Japanese diplomatic traffic. However, the military commanders in Southeast Asia had little faith in these new forms of intelligence gathering and disregarded much of the contents of the daily situation reports.

Despite FECB intercepts on an imminent Japanese invasion, Brooke-Popham announced that Japan could not go to War before February 1942.

In general, Malaya Command's intelligence unit relied on the local intelligence branches of the civilian police and its remit was only to cover what was happening within the country. As such the General Staff Officer (Intelligence) for Malaya Command produced an appreciation of situation arguing that Japanese forces could not land on the east coast of the Malay Peninsula in the monsoon then prevailing and that there was only one road down the peninsula, which could be held by two battalions. More importantly, it noted that tanks could not be used in the country.

Brooke-Popham, Percival and his fellow Generals, who had access to the "Y" and intelligence intercepts from the FECB, clearly failed to grasp the importance of the information they were provided with. Even if they did, their actions showed that the information they had received was obviously rejected in the decisions they made.

The FECB had found a Japanese spy holed up in Singapore. Through intercepts, it had determined that a Japanese Major General was concealed in the Japanese Consul's office in Singapore as a "language officer who reported closely upon the numbers and efficiency of the British forces there. Apparently also the correspondence with him included an outline of the plans forecast and estimates of the length of time and strength necessary to knock out certain defensive positions"[6]

The intercepts, which had been translated verbatim and were filled with flowery Japanese speech, was sent to Malaya Command. Instead of acting on the report, the officer in charge poked fun at the flowery speech and refused to take the report seriously.

Again from diplomatic sources (intercepted diplomatic telegrams from Tokyo) the FECB informed Malaya Command of the Japanese arrangements for notifying their decision to commence hostilities. The words "East Wind" and "West Wind" appearing at the end of certain broadcasts meant that it had been decided to break off relations with the US (East), USSR (North), UK (West).[7]

FECB urgently alerted Hong Kong and the Americans at Corregidor to this message but it was Hong Kong who first heard the fateful message on 7 December 1941. On that day, as Japan geared up for its attack on the American Fleet in Pearl Harbour and British forces in Malaya, the Japanese diplomatic and consular messages between Tokyo, the Philippines, Malaya and the Netherlands East Indies, which had formed the bulk of diplomatic special intelligence for the FECB, suddenly ceased.

A few months earlier, the Japanese had also changed its JN25 code, the main code used by the Japanese military in communicating with its units. Through a lack of staff and machinery, the JN25 code was left to Bletchley Park and Washington. Days before the Japanese invasion, they changed their fleet code. So by the evening of the 7th, FECB was unable to read the Japanese air, army and fleet signals and all diplomatic signals, which they had previously been intercepting, had also stopped.

However, this in itself should have been a big enough warning for the generals at Malaya Command that the Japanese attack was imminent.

Just before Pearl Harbour in Hawaii was attacked at 3:25am on 8 December 1941(Tokyo time), the Japanese 25th Army's 18th Division had already landed at Kota Bahru in Northern Malaya at 2:15am. Another Japanese Division, the 5th, landed in Singora and Pattani in Southern Thailand at 4am.

The Japanese landings at Kota Bahru were met with stiff resistance. These landings marked the start of the Malayan Campaign, the Japanese planned conquest of Malaya.

The Japanese plan was to capture Singapore, where the British naval base and the headquarters of the British Army were located. On the same day, 17 Japanese navy bombers flying from Saigon (now Ho Chi Minh City), attacked the Keppel Harbour docks, the Naval Base in Sembawang as well as the Seletar and Tengah air bases in Singapore. The "Y" station, which had been keeping a 24-hour watch, gave the warning at 0345hours of the pending air attack over Singapore. The top-secret radar facilities, had also been tracking the large number of Japanese aircraft and provided a warning of a large convoy of unidentified planes headed for Singapore. However, the Governor Shenton Thomas' decision to withhold permission to sound the air raid sirens without his explicit permission meant that the sirens came on only after some of the first bombs had hit Singapore. The lights of the city were ablaze as the official responsible had taken home the keys to the light switch boxes.

Following the outbreak of hostilities, it was recommended that the Commanders at Singapore should receive all the aid they needed for the defence of Singapore and the army and RAF had enough "Y" operators in Singapore to receive and translate the necessary Japanese army and air traffic.

However, the lack of cooperation from the navy, the naval extended defence office at the Battlebox and the new combined air and army Headquarters at Sime Road meant that a naval disaster that could have been prevented, was about to occur.

At dusk on 8 December, the Prince of Wales and the Repulse, two capital ships and Singapore's main naval strength, also known as Force Z, left for their ill-fated journey to intercept the Japanese landings in Malaya. A trip which left more than 800 Allied sailors dead and the two ships sunk when Japanese fighters intercepted and dive bombed the two ships and their escort vessels off Kuantan on 10 December, marking the end of the naval war in the campaign just two days after hostilities began.

The two ships were alongside the main wharf and could be seen from the FECB's offices at the Naval Base on 8 December. However, the two ships disappeared on the 9 December and that visual disappearance was the last bit of information the FECB had on the two ships. The FECB had earlier given notice of a Japanese fleet off the South China Sea and this was what the ships had gone to investigate. However, no one at the Battlebox or Combined headquarters had told the FECB that Force Z had been scrambled to meet this threat. Not keeping the FECB informed about ongoing operations meant that the signal intelligence officers were not overly concerned about a Japanese report in P/L (plain language) on 10 December, which said British capital ships were sighted at a specific position off Kuantan. Although Malaya Command and the

Admiralty were informed immediately, no one at these headquarters had pieced the two together and realised that Japanese fighters had obviously spotted Force Z and were now planning to destroy it. Had the FECB been kept in the loop, it is highly likely that defensive air cover would have been sent sooner to aid the capital ships, rather than after receiving distress calls from the floundering vessels.

The Japanese decision to use plain language for operational purposes in emergencies was also surprising as it was expected that they would always communicate in code. As a result, a linguist was continually on duty at the "Y" station in Kranji to deal immediately with such intercepts. This was good news.

> They reported that three new uncyphered codes, apparently naval, air division and air to ground , were being used extensively by the Japanese during operations and they thought it was very promising and they also noted that Jap. P/L (plain language) sighting reports of our forces were invaluable — Interpreters were continually on duty at the W/T station and passed information by telephone to the War Room (at the Combined Headquarters at Sime Road). [8]

However, the intelligence gained was sent to COIS, which felt it was of a low grade and did not need to be distributed to the Commanders-in-Chief. This meant that the Commanders-in-Chief were kept out of the loop on many of the signals coups achieved by "Y" station.

Moreover, with the failure to activate Operation Matador early enough to forestall the Japanese in Thai territory, the British high command gave the enemy enough time to build a beach head and land an attacking force that pushed hard against the British defenders.

The confusion in the first few days, which led to many retreats, marked how the British would fight the entire campaign.

The level of confusion and the lack of information in the rear headquarters verged almost on the comical. Unclear orders and diversions of troops meant that military communications in Malaya were affected. There were insufficient secure telephone lines from III Indian Corps in Kuala Lumpur to the combined headquarters at Sime Road and Headquarters Malaya Command at Fort Canning. As a result, it was impossible to get updated reports on what was happening in northern Malaya. Some of the forward field headquarters of the various fighting divisions which relayed reports to their corps headquarters in Kuala Lumpur were unable to get a response on further directions from Heath as Heath was unable to get in touch with Percival in Singapore in order for strategic decisions to be made:

> ...We turned up at the signal office (Kuala Lumpur) and found a situation of almost panic. All the lights on the sixty line switchboard were lit and waiting to be put through and the only direct line to Singapore was not being used. A call from General Percival to be put through on the scrambler phone to HQ Far East had been kept waiting as the new man did not know how to initiate such a call. [9]

As a result, the new combined headquarters, with limited communication lines and working with inexperienced staff up-country posed a serious problem from the start. Thus, this lack of a proper command, control and communications setup contributed in part to the daily losses faced by the British.

The situation at the Battlebox had also become more complicated with new anti-aircraft gun positions being set up as old ones were captured by the enemy. By the middle of December, Fortress Signals had to install a fourth multiphone at the Gun Operations Room to accommodate three new gun positions. [10]

As the overall operational headquarters in Malaya, the combined headquarters at Sime Road should have been at the centre of command, control and communications. Instead, the commanders had huge difficulty even determining what was happening on the ground and then even more problems in issuing orders. Often, Percival would have to drive all the way up to Kuala Lumpur in order to consult with Heath and shape the direction of the battles. With overloaded communications facilities, it was not until the end of December that Fortress Signals set up three new 7-pair cables from Sime Road to the Bukit Timah exchange[11] in order to ease the signals traffic situation and provide enough signal lines for Combined headquarters to communicate directly with other divisional and corps headquarters in the field rather than through the Fort Canning exchange.

The idea of a combined headquarters, which Percival had pushed through, was, in theory, sound:

A large room where the army and air force staffs could work at Sime Road adjoining R.A.F. Headquarters. On the other side of it were built offices for the Army operational staff. The idea was that the staff officers of the two services and their clerks should all work in the Combined Operations Room, though they had their own rooms to which they could go if they wanted to. This was excellent in theory. In practice, it had many faults. It meant that our staff officers were permanently in that room because they could not in fact work in two places. That in turn meant that their clerks were permanently there too and — worse than that — it meant that the commanders had to spend much of their time there, so as to be close to their staff officers. Had we worked entirely in our own offices, either we or our staff officers would have been faced with a journey of a hundred yards or so every time we wanted to talk to each other — and that during the black-out was not too pleasant.[12]

More importantly, the newly built huts and facilities for the combined headquarters suffered from shoddy workmanship and poor planning. There was a lack of desk and planning areas as well as effective ventilation and cooling machines:

The conditions in the Combined Operations Room were not conducive to good work or clear thinking. They were too cramped and there was too much noise. The problem may not arise again in these days of integrated staffs, but I am sure the right solution in those conditions is for staffs to work in their own offices and to have a common room where everything of interest to all Services, i.e. situation maps, intelligence reports, messages, etc., can be seen, and where conferences can be held. It may seem a small point to some, but I feel sure that all who have had experience of the working of headquarter staffs will agree with me that the conditions under which they work have a very great influence on their efficiency and, in consequence, on the efficiency of the fighting formations which they direct. [13]

The stresses of an inadequate headquarters and war operations room clearly handicapped British decision making and the large time lags in giving instructions would have in part led to early retreats by inexperienced troops, who could not wait for instructions that may or may not have even been received by their commanders in the rear.

By Christmas Day 1941, Hong Kong had fallen and the Japanese had seized all Malayan territory lying north and west of the Perak River.

This included Penang Island, the states of Perlis, Kedah, Kelantan and a greater part of Perak.

They had also destroyed the backbone of the RAF squadrons and seized all its northern airstrips, thanks in no small measure to a British traitor based at the Alor Star airfield who conveyed flight and attack plans to the Japanese via a secret wireless transmitter.

By the time he was caught, Captain P.S.V. Heenan had contributed significantly to the huge loss of RAF aircraft and northern airfields in the theatre. The airfields would never be recaptured.[14]

It was a losing battle all the way down the peninsula and by 30 January, the retreat of the British and Commonwealth troops were almost complete with the loss of the whole of Malaya. Piped across by Highland bagpipers, the Argyll and Sutherland Higlanders slow march across the causeway linking the Malayan mainland to the island of Singapore, marked the end of the battle for Malaya and the start of the battle for Singapore.

By January, the FECB had also packed up most of its kit and were preparing to sail off for Colombo, in anticipation of the fall of Singapore. Major John Westall, a Royal Marine Staff Officer (Intelligence) at the signals office in the Naval Base noted that Japanese, "naval intelligence was unobtainable by the end of Jan 1942. All reporting officers had fled or been captured... FECB had left for Colombo and Staff Officer (Intelligence) Singapore was mainly engaged on liaison with the civil authorities" [15]

In defence of the intelligence officers, he pointed out that the giving out of a general and effective warning of impeding Japanese attack was the responsibility of the FECB and this is what they did. They also warned about the departure of a big Japanese convoy which Admiral Tom Phillips and Force Z (*HMS Prince of Wales* and *HMS Repulse*) had attempted to intercept before they met their end on 10 December:

> Further action would have been taken on these reports had it not been for the fact that up-to-date information from these — 'particularly sources' was treated as being so secret that no action could be taken.[16]

> The FECB had left two interpreters, Colgrave and Cooper, along with minimal equipment, to provide air intelligence while the rest of the team evacuated. Cooper started to work on Japanese naval air R/T (radio transmissions).

He proved that it could be taken and used and was drafted into carrying out watches with Colgrave at the headphone. Cooper, who had lived in Japan found the work comparatively easy. Japanese security was not high and after study of bomber radio transmissions they were able to elicit that formations, recognizable by some sort of unchanging pet names, specialised upon certain targets. Thus when the unit airborne was recognised its probable target could be foretold, while from counting the number of individual calls and acknowledgements the strength of the forces airborne could be assessed. Results were telephoned to the local RAF defence and several successful actions were fought, when after the first two or three days the RAF learnt to rely upon the accuracy of this information. A certain small amount of low-grade cipher was taken and read but R/T were the thing.[17]

However, this intelligence information proved to be too little, too late. The RAF in Malaya had been effectively destroyed, thanks to Japanese attacks and Captain Heenan's treachery. It was now an issue of how to prevent an even greater loss of lives and destruction of military forces. The RAF finally, through the combined operations headquarters in Sime Road, began providing this signals intelligence to the various anti-aircraft batteries throughout Malaya. Although it was sporadic, the information did help to partially counter some air attacks. This, however, remained more the exception than the rule.

However, very little of this signals intelligence actually reached the Commanders in Chief. After the fall of Singapore, Vice Admiral Sir Geoffrey Layton, the Commander-in-Chief, China Fleet (to whom FECB reported to in Singapore) had escaped to Ceylon along with the rest of the bureau. He gave the outfit a week to come up with useful information or be shut down. Layton commented that the two officers left in Singapore had come up with more results than the bureau put together. Layton had never received the extensive intelligence findings that the FECB had given to Malaya Command nor was he made aware of the bureau's warnings about the *Prince of Wales* and *Repulse*. As COIS had filtered most of the reports to Layton, it was ironic that the unit which provided so much useful intelligence was now going to be shut for not allegedly providing any information.[18]

By 31 January 1942, Johore state was in the hands of the Japanese. The retreating forces blew up the Causeway behind them creating a

60-yard gap, but this was quickly repaired by Japanese engineers by 11 February and was used to bring tanks and mechanised vehicles onto the island.

One of the reasons for the swift descent of Japanese troops down Malaya was their ingenious use of bicycles and boats made of light steel and Kapok wood, many of which were confiscated from the local population.

Moreover, the Japanese, after campaigns in China and additional training, were better suited to the climate and ate off the land as opposed to the Allied troops, many of whom had only recently been in-country and did not eat the local food which was rice-based.

The Japanese also used old roads and paths in the jungles to outflank most of the Allied troops who guarded the main north-south road and left their sides exposed. By using small boats, the Japanese were able to land behind the British troops and create confusion in rear areas causing the British to retreat further.

As the British had lost most of their naval elements and the RAF almost non-existent after the first week of war, their positions were easily strafed and most troop movements had to be done in the cover of darkness.

The Japanese use of armour in the form of tanks allowed them to plough through the weak British defences and race down the peninsula, with the allies in full retreat.

As lines of communications were destroyed, it was hard to determine what was happening in the front lines and junior officers made tactical and strategic withdrawal decisions without consulting senior commanders, leading to missing units and a very confused picture of the war on the plotting tables at the combined headquarters in Singapore.

Before the Japanese invasion in late 1941, Percival had ignored all proposals by Simson to shore up the northern defences of Singapore. Simson pointed out that all the fixed defences were guarding the south against an invasion from the sea. He was quite sure that the Japanese assault would come from the north, across the straits instead.

However, Percival felt that it was bad for the morale of the troops and civilians if such measures were taken. Percival also believed that the Japanese assault, if it came from the north, would come from the northeast where four batteries of 6- and 15-inch guns provided firepower. This thinking differed from his original assessment as a staff officer in Malaya Command in the 1930s when he predicted an attack from the northwest. His original assessment would prove prophetic. Thus, Singapore was deprived of solid northern defences.

Till late 1941, everyone believed that Singapore, the "Impregnable fortress" would not be affected by the war. She was protected from the north by thick Malayan jungles and from the south by coastal guns, spotted all along the eastern and south western coasts of Singapore. Troop reinforcements and the arrival of the Prince of Wales and the Repulse lulled the people into feeling that the British could easily drive off the Japanese.

Percival had about 80,000 troops which were disposed all over peninsular Malaya in fortified positions, guarding airfields and important installations. He had no tanks (only light gun carriers) and 150 obsolete planes. His navy had suffered a great loss with the sinking of the *Prince of Wales* and the *Repulse*. Britain had no ships left to send down to Singapore and the attack on the American Pacific fleet at Pearl Harbor meant that the US had no major battleships in the region that could assist the British.

The Japanese 25th Army — comprising the 5th, 18th and Imperial Guards Division — had about 67,000 men with 150 tanks and 560 first line aircraft. Though smaller in number in terms of men, it had superior air support, naval elements and tanks.

Besides the British troops, Singapore's local units consisted of four battalions of the Straits Settlements Volunteer Corps and a small civil defence force. With the impending Japanese attack, the Chinese put aside their various differences and offered their services to the Governor, Sir Shenton Thomas. As a result, the Chinese National Council was formed on 31 December 1941 under the leadership of Tan Kah Kee, a prominent businessman.

Receiving enthusiastic support, the council, through volunteers like Lim Bo Seng, organised labour forces to maintain essential services and construct defence works. Selected members were trained for combat and guerrilla warfare in Japanese-occupied territories. Soon they became the pioneering members of the Malayan People's Anti-Japanese Army.

As the Japanese gathered on the banks of the Johore Straits before beginning their invasion of the island, Percival's plan for the defence of Singapore was to divide the country into three defence sectors. Heath was put in command of the northern sector with the British 18th Division, the Indian 11th and 9th Divisions under his command; Major General Gordon Bennett, Commander of the Australian Imperial Forces, was in charge of the western sector with his fresh Australian troops and the untrained Indian 44th Infantry Brigade under his command; Simmons took care of the southern sector, with the 1st and 2nd Malaya Infantry Regiment, the Straits Settlements Volunteer Force, fortress troops and fixed defences under his charge.

Bennett's defence of the 4.5 mile northwest coastline, stretching from Kranji River to Sarimbun River, was very weak. It was far too extended for his troops, numbering around 750 men. The mangrove swamps and the heavy jungle prohibited construction of defence obstacles. This was to prove fatal.

At Kluang, Johore, on 1 February 1942, Lieutenant General Tomoyuki Yamashita, the Commander of the Japanese forces in the Malayan Campaign, revealed his assault plans to his commanders. The initial thrust would be aimed at the north-western shoreline. He tasked the 5th and 18th Divisions for the job. The Imperial Guards Division would create a diversion in the east (Pulau Ubin) to fool Malaya Command, and heavy artillery bombardment would be directed along the entire northern sector of Singapore to conceal the actual landing areas.

After securing a foothold in Singapore, Yamashita's first task was to capture Tengah airfield, followed by the capture of Mandai village. The next target was to be the Bukit Timah high ground and then to the Seletar, Pierce and MacRitchie reservoirs. Yamashita hoped to cut off the water supply to the island and force an early surrender of the British.

Meanwhile, the Japanese air force, free to roam Singapore's skies, raided the Royal Navy's oil storage tanks at the Naval Base, sending huge columns of dense black smoke into the air. They also attacked the Tanjong Pagar railway station.

Japanese intelligence dispatched two teams of swimmers across the straits on 3 February to gather information on the Australian artillery and troop positions. They reported back after three days with very accurate sketches.

On 6 February, Yamashita shifted his headquarters to the Sultan of Johore's Palace at Bukit Serene. This provided him with a good view of the key targets, only a mile away across the Straits. The Palace was never harassed by the Australians who were guarding that sector because it was the ancestral home of their old friend Sultan Ibrahim, who was very close to Bennett. Any damage to his residence would have had extensive repercussions to these ties.

Soon after nightfall on 7 February, 1942, 400 men of the Japanese Imperial Guards Division landed and occupied Pulau Ubin in a feint attack. They encountered minimum resistance. Though large troop movements in the Johore rubber plantations across from the north western sector of Singapore had been sighted earlier, no action was taken as Percival received the intelligence report only hours before the attack.

The Japanese artillery began intensive firing and Japanese planes also began bombing the military headquarters within the western sector. Telegraph and telephone communications were destroyed in this bombardment. By nightfall, communications throughout the northwest defence areas were in shambles and communications between the front line and command headquarters were broken.

On the night of 8 February, Japanese troops of the 5th and 18th Division began to cross the Straits using sea craft hidden near the water's edge. These were launched in the backwaters of the Skudai, Danga, Perpet and Melayu rivers. This first assault was repelled by Australian machine-gunners, but other sea craft were able to seek and infiltrate gaps in the defence line.

By the third wave, the Australians were outnumbered and over-whelmed as machine gunners soon ran out of ammunition and the troops were crippled by the breakdown of communications with their command headquarters. At midnight, a red star shell burst over the Straits indicating to Yamashita the 5th Division's successful landing on Singapore soil. A white star shell burst later, to confirm the 18th Division's successful infiltration.

The Australians were unable to hold back the Japanese advance towards Tengah airfield for long. The Australian commander, Brigadier H.B. Taylor, planned to counterattack the Japanese's two-pronged movement towards Lim Chu Kang Rd and Choa Chu Kang Rd, but was foiled as the frontline troops were in disarray. He endeavoured to form a defence line running down Lim Chu Kang Rd to its junction with Choa Chu Kang Rd and westwards to Choa Chu Kang village. However, heavy artillery fire and Japanese air bombardment forced him to withdraw to the Kranji-Jurong line on the afternoon of 9 February.

The Kranji-Jurong Line was an arbitrary line drawn from Kranji river to Jurong river. Loss of areas along this line meant that the Japanese would be able to advance down to the city from the west and through Bukit Timah Road.

Due to the importance of this line, Percival ordered reinforcements to the Bukit Panjang-Keat Hong Road junction to the right of the line. One Australian brigade was to remain holding the Causeway sector while

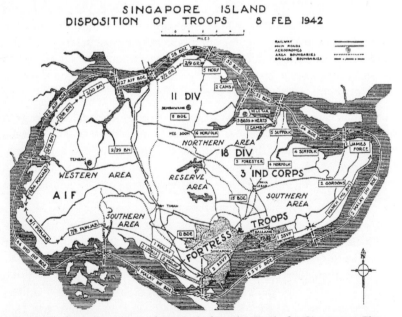

Percival's final disposition of troops before the Battle for Singapore. The Australians in the northwest would face the brunt of the enemy invasion.

another brigade would try to stabilise the Kranji-Jurong Line. The 44th Indian Brigade in the west was also withdrawn to the left of the Kranji-Jurong Line while another Indian Brigade was to move to the Bukit Timah race course to protect the island's vital food and petrol supplies located nearby.

However, Percival knew this might not be enough to hold back the Japanese and made preparations for a last desperate stand. He planned to hold a perimeter covering Kallang aerodrome, MacRitchie and Pierce reservoirs and the Bukit Timah supply depot area. He issued this instruction in secret to his three commanders. But these instructions were soon to be misunderstood by Taylor.

On 10 February, the Japanese suffered one of their major losses at the Kranji river. The Imperial Guards while moving up the Kranji river at midnight, got bogged down in the mangrove swamps and lost in the tributaries. Many died when Australian soldiers set fire to oil from demolished fuel tanks which gushed into the waterways burning everything in sight.

General Nishimura, the commander of the Imperial Guards, in panic, wanted permission to withdraw but was reprimanded by Yamashita. However, through a misunderstanding of orders, the Australians started withdrawing from the causeway sector, giving the invaders the liberty to move further inland.

It was at this time that Yamashita first stepped onto Singapore island in the predawn darkness and set up his mobile headquarters in a rubber plantation just north of Tengah airfield.

Over at the Kranji-Jurong Line, Taylor who received a coded signal modified by Bennett, regarding Percival's last stand plans, misread them. He took it as an instruction to head immediately to the defence perimeter positions. This set in motion a series of related withdrawals from the northern sector of the Kranji-Jurong Line which allowed the Japanese to swiftly take control of Woodlands Road.

At 1:30pm on the same day, the 44th Indian Brigade was also in full retreat from the southern extreme of the Kranji-Jurong Line following clashes with Japanese infantry units and having suffered heavy air and artillery bombardment. Through a series of miscalculations and miscommunication, the Kranji-Jurong Line was wrested away from the British by mid-afternoon.

Japanese tanks also made their first appearance on the island on 10 February. They were floated across the Straits to Lim Chu Kang Road early in the day, and joined in the battle at dusk. They made their way down Choa Chu Kang Road and stopped at the Bukit Panjang Village and Bukit Timah Road junction to wait for more ammunition supplies and support artillery. The Australian troops were no match for the tanks and fled to the hills east of Bukit Panjang Village.

11 February 1942 was Kigensetsu, the anniversary celebration of the coronation of Emperor Jimmu who founded the Chrysanthemum throne and began the present dynasty. This was also the day Yamashita had hoped to capture Singapore.

Ammunition supplies were running low for the Japanese forces. He had letters dropped over Headquarters Malaya Command areas urging Percival to give up his desperate fight, hoping for an early surrender.

It was also on the morning of 11 February that Percival finally moved his Combined Operations Headquarters from the compound in Sime Road back to the Battlebox at Fort Canning. With this, he abandoned his home at Flagstaff House and would, from now, be sleeping in his above ground office at Fort Canning. Four days later, it would all be over.

> At 6am on the eleventh, after a few hours' sleep at Sime Road, I woke up to the sounds of machine-gun fire. Thinking it was probably only some anti-aircraft fire, I sent my A.D.C., Stonor of the Argylls, who had been untiring in his efforts to help me the whole campaign, out to investigate. He soon came back saying there appeared to be a battle going on beyond the end of the golf-course about a mile from where we were. I thought it was time to move. We had prepared an alternative headquarters on Thomson Road but there was no point in going there now, so I decided to join rear headquarters at Fort Canning.[19]

At the Battlebox, the situation had become confused as the whole of the Combined headquarters along with air liaison elements shifted their operations into the complex. Air Headquarters had decided to move to 300 Thomson Road but by 12 February, was already overrun. With that the RAF's role came to a final halt in Singapore.

By now, there was not much of the battle left to direct out of the Battlebox. The whole of Malaya had been lost and more than half of Singapore island had already been occupied by the advancing Japanese. It was now just delaying tactics. As the staff officers and planners shifted, the joint operations room and communications facilities were blown up at Sime Road. (However, the Sime Road complex would still play a role in the lives of captured British civilians in Singapore. In the middle of the Japanese Occupation, the huts that made up the combined operations headquarters, were converted into a civilian internment camp. The European civilian population, which had till then been housed at the civilian prison in Changi, were shifted to Sime Road in order to make more room for the surviving Allied POWs who had returned after building the Thai-Burma Death railway. Governor Shenton Thomas' wife, Lady Thomas, was also interned at the Sime Road camp.)

At Fort Canning's Battlebox, the Plotting Room (which had now been taken over by the General Staff) and the Gun Operations Room became the main operational rooms as the combined headquarters had now been reduced to directing the last bits of fighting on the island.

There was an excess of staff with no particular role to play.

> Accommodation there was very congested as Headquarters Southern Area and Anti-Aircraft Defences were also there. The General Staff went into the bomb-proof shelter which had been constructed before the war. It was never meant to hold as many bodies as this and the ventilating arrangements were inadequate. In consequence, the staff room became terribly hot and the staff worked under most unpleasant conditions.[20]

Although the main above ground building was never directly hit, the shells fired by Japanese artillery came very close. Most of the officers and staff were now camped out at the headquarters with several adjoining houses requisitioned as mess halls to feed the large numbers now at Fort Canning.

Eric Lomax, a signaller, who survived the war, described the last days in the Battlebox.

> ...This was the 'Battlebox'. I went in and didn't come out for three weeks. The siege of Singapore for me was a series of clipped shouts for help over the radio and terse bulletins of disaster...

...I spent most of my time underground in the Battlebox, hearing and relaying orders, passing on information, sending out instructions for desperate recombinations of units to try to stop the collapse...

...Not that I saw daylight much: we worked eighteen hours a day, and slept on the floor of the command centre among the radios and phones. Our offices were a series of connecting rooms, so that runners and despatch riders were always coming through and stepping over tired bodies. We saw nothing until the very end, and what we heard was confused. We knew that the Japanese had taken the reservoirs and turned off the taps; we could hear their unchallenged planes bombing and strafing every day. The big ships were leaving Keppel Harbour with civilians; troops were deserting and wandering around the city. Towards the end the commanders couldn't even give sensible orders because there was so little information coming in. I saw General Percival a few times, walking in a corridor of the Fort or through our signals centre, a gaunt, tall figure looking utterly dejected and crushed; he was already a broken man. He was about to have his name attached to the worst defeat in the British Army's history.[21]

A day earlier, Wavell, visited Singapore for a 24-hour visit to assess the situation. He had taken over from Brooke-Popham in early January 1942 and was now Commander-in-Chief, South West Pacific Command, which covered the Malayan theatre and the Dutch East Indies. He was not impressed by what he saw in Singapore. Churchill had urged that, "Commanders and senior officers should die with their troops" and that "It is expected that every unit will be brought into close contact with the enemy and fight it out".[22]

However, it was clear to Wavell that the men were demoralised and it was unlikely that Percival could produce a more "offensive spirit and optimistic outlook" among the men. Before leaving, Wavell scribbled down an Order of the Day, which was to be sent out by the signals at Sime Road. The message read:

It is certain that our troops in Singapore Island greatly outnumber any Japanese who have crossed the straits. We must destroy them.

Our fighting reputation is at stake and the honour of the British Empire. The Americans have held out in the Bataan Peninsula against far heavier odds, the Russians are turning back the packed strength of the Germans, the Chinese with an almost complete lack of modern equipment have held the Japanese for four-and-a half years. It would be disgraceful if we yield our boasted fortress of Singapore to inferior forces.

There must be no thought of sparing the troops or the civilian population and no mercy must be shown to any weakness. Commanders and senior officers must lead their troops and if necessary, die with them. Every unit must fight it out to the end and in close contact with the enemy.

Please see that the above is brought to the notice of all senior officers and by them to the troops.

I look upon you and your men to fight it to the end and prove that the fighting spirit that won our Empire still exists to enable us to defend us.[23]

The Order was given to Percival just before Wavell left early in the morning of 11 February. While boarding his Sunderland seaplane in the dark, Wavell fell from the quay and broke two small bones in his back. As a result, for the next crucial four days, the most senior commander running the War in Malaya was doing it from bed.

Percival planned to transmit Wavell's Order of the Day in the morning of 11 February but because his Sime Road headquarters retreated to the Battlebox, was unable to issue his and Wavell's directive until late afternoon. By then, Percival's order to the men were no more than just words:

...In units the troops have not shown the fighting spirit which is expected of men of the British Empire. It will be a lasting disgrace to us if we are to be defeated by an Army of clever gangsters our inferior numbers in strength.

The spirit of aggression and determination to stick it out must be inculcated to all ranks. There must be no further withdrawals without orders. There are too many fighting men roving about the back areas. Every available man who is not on essential work must be used to stop the invaders.[24]

With the collapse of the Kranji-Jurong Line, the Imperial Guards started to move down to their target, the MacRitchie and Pierce reservoirs. They had also managed to repair the causeway by now and began moving more tanks, men and equipment across.

The defending troops, by this time were badly demoralised. Thousands of exhausted and frightened stragglers left the fighting to seek shelter in large commercial buildings.

On 12 February, the defenders clashed with Japanese troops at Bukit Timah Road, south of Bukit Timah Village, Nee Soon Village and Pasir Panjang.

Over at the general staff operations room in the Battlebox, Percival marked out Singapore's final protective perimeter. It was 28 miles long enclosing Kallang airfield, Thomson village, Macritchie reservoir, Adam Rd, Farrer, Holland and Bouna Vista Roads.

By this time, Singapore was already coming under heavy air attack with almost daily bombings by Japanese aircraft. Royal Navy officer David Copley noted that when Fort Canning came under attack by aerial bombs and field artillery, the General Staff (Intelligence) clerks were made to destroy every document in the Battlebox and above ground buildings, including archives going back a few decades. Lorry loads of documents were sent to the municipal refuse incinerator until it was overrun by the Japanese. Those that were too sensitive were fed page by page into fires in local clay cooking stoves on the balconies. Smoke from these fires could be seen drifting across Fort Canning, darkening the already smoky air. According to Copley, who was involved in the destruction of documents, navy coders also destroyed their books outside the Battlebox:

> So one day towards the end, a most urgent, most severe message came to the GOC Malaya from General Wavell just after the had visited Singapore and returned to India (sic). The GOC and his staff could not decipher the message because the books had been destroyed because of the nearness of the Japanese and similarly the naval authorities had no cipher or code books still undestroyed.[25]

Eventually, a code book was found to decode Wavell's order but it was clear that no one expected the defenders to hold on for much longer.

On 13 February, Yamashita moved his headquarters forward to the bomb-damaged Ford Motor factory. He feared a prolonged war once Percival had dug in at his last defensive position to wait for relief reinforcements. He had not enough men or ammunition for a long war.

Thus, he tasked the 18th Division to capture Alexandra Barracks and the Imperial Guards to capture MacRitchie quickly before Percival had settled in at his last stand. The massacre at the Alexandra Military Hospital was a result of the 18th Division's attack, with innocent doctors and nurses killed as they tried to save patients on the operating table. Japanese soldiers bayoneted the staff and patients alike, killing over 200 in the hospital.[26]

Hordes of people had already begun trying to evacuate from Singapore in whatever vessels they could find. As women and children tried to board ships destined for Australia and India, unruly troops who had abandoned their units tried to get on board the ships in order to escape the island. Many of the ships which were packed to the gunnels did not make it, not because of the number of people aboard, but because they were bombed and attacked by Japanese aircraft as they tried to flee the island.

Many essential staff and personnel lost their lives during the evacuations. Top Secret documents and vast gold bullion from the Straits Settlements treasury that were being shipped off the island were also lost when the ships carrying them were sunk by the Japanese fleet off the Singapore coast.

Many fleeing vessels managed to get through the Japanese blockade to the islands off the Netherlands East Indies (present day Indonesia) and escaped but the remaining stragglers were eventually caught by the Japanese within a month of the fall of Singapore.

It was at Pasir Panjang that the 1st and 2nd Battalion Malay Regiment began their epic 48-hour stand against the Japanese. They held on stubbornly while others along the lines were toppling. Only when the regiment was almost wiped out to a man was the ridge given up.

Over at the Battlebox in Fort Canning, the lack of information was deafening as the operations room did not have an accurate update of what was happening outside the war rooms. Pleas for help and reinforcements as well as blood-curdling screams were heard over the radio as the hapless residents of the bunker tried in vain to communicate with units being destroyed by enemy shelling and attacks.

In a meeting in the underground complex, Heath and Bennett urged Percival to surrender as the civilian toll was mounting while the troops were too exhausted, demoralised and disorganised to continue. Percival, however, still refused to yield. The recently decoded message from Wavell had instructed Percival to fight to the last and give no consideration to any other factors. Percival said that he had his honour to consider and the question as to what posterity would think if they surrendered the large army and fortress. To this, Heath commented dryly, "You need not bother about your honour. You lost that a long time ago up in the North." Plans were drawn up for the evacuation of key personnel but only a few would survive the tightening noose of Japanese warships in the waters surrounding Singapore.[27]

14 February dawned bitterly on the defending forces. The Japanese 18th division continued their assault on the besieged Malay regiment and the Imperial Guards Division swarmed out of the MacRitchie area to battle the Allied forces. Water failure was imminent and epidemic threatened the overpopulated city.

Wavell, safely ensconced in his Java headquarters, sent Churchill a telegram indicating that the end for Singapore was very near:

> Have received telegram from Percival that enemy are close to town and that his troops are incapable of further counter-attack. Have ordered him to continue inflict maximum damage to enemy by house-to-house fighting if necessary. Fear however that resistance not likely to be very prolonged.[28]

Wavell wanted permission to allow Percival to surrender and Churchill gave it to him:

> You are of course sole judge of the moment when no further result can be gained at Singapore, and should instruct Percival accordingly, C.I.G.S. concurs.[29]

This signal marked the final play in Singapore's death pangs as Wavell now could give Percival the permission he so desperately sought in order to end the continuing slaughter. However, Wavell would wait till the morning of 15 February before conveying this permission

For the civilian population, it seemed to be the end of the world. The city had been devastated by bombings, the constant air raid sirens and the artillery barrages which made the town look like a scene out of Dante's *Inferno*.

For the few remaining civilians that were still manning at the various public services, it was a very trying time. Cuthbert Oswald Donough, a local Eurasian boy, was working for the Cable and Wireless office at Robinson Road. C&W was the civilian cable office, from which urgent signals, military and civilian, were still being sent to London and various other parts of Southeast Asia as the city collapsed outside its walls.

By 12 February, C&W was still able to transmit signals via its underground submarine cables to Banjoewangie, East Java, via the Cocos islands to Cottesloe, Western Australia and then to South Africa through to London. All acceptance counters for telegrams were closed to the public and the Phonogram (telephone) service was suspended. Only government, military and press messages were accepted for submission as all clerical staff except those in the operating and engineering departments were released from duty. There was so much confusion that even secret and sensitive military signals, that could not be sent through the Battlebox's signals office because of the heavily choked circuits, were sent by dispatch riders to the C&W office, where they were then sent via civilian cable lines to London. The C&W office acted as a secondary signal office for Malaya Command and a teletype between Fortress Signals and C&W was operational right to the very end.

A small unit of RAF signalers, believed to be the remnants of the radar unit, had also shifted from their base to the C&W's Robinson Road offices and had set up their own circuits there in a bid to make contact with their units in Java. Although they were unsuccessful, they remained camped in the ground floor offices of the C&W as upstairs, Donough and his colleagues were furiously dispatching the last signals out of Singapore:

> Then came that fateful Friday, 13 February. (C&W's) General Supervisor A.G. Blackwell came to the office in the early morning. He took down the names of staff working in the Instrument Room (operating staff) and Control Room (technical staff), he then sent a message himself and destroyed the punched slip. He told us he was leaving and we would close down the circuits and go home. As he left, I called out to Ronnie Barth who was standing close to the outgoing monitor, which was still switched on, to read from the outgoing slip what Blackwell had sent. Barth read out, "To MD/ London, Now closing down. Goodbye. Most unlikely able evacuate please inform wives". [30]

As they had not received any instructions from Fort Canning, Donough thought it strange that the circuits should be shut down. With hundreds of urgent telegrams that had to be sent before the city fell, Donough and his colleagues decided to rebel:

> I punched an XQ (circuit route) on a KBP (keyboard perforator) and rushed it off on the Batavia (Jakarta) /Banjoewangi circuit saying, "Please keep circuit open.Staff still on duty." Ronnie Barth, Dick Lesslar, Ken De Souza, Bruce Armstrong and I decided that we would stay on till the end.
>
> That morning the ack-ack (anti-aircraft) gun positions just behind our office building was bombed in an air raid. The guns were destroyed and the gunners killed. Then came repeated raids by fighter planes, machine gunning our building. We were thankful that our window panes were made of solid steel. The noise was both deafening and terrifying. At about noon, our building was bombed. The bomb fell on the rooftop but did not penetrate the roof. The other went through the air-well. The damage was not serious — only the Battery Room and the Carpenter's Workshop were affected...
>
> ...Later that afternoon, an army major came with orders that we must destroy all the transmitting and receiving equipment in his presence. We protested but to no avail. We took heavy tools from the workshop and smashed all the transmitting and receiving automatic equipment. After the officer left, Bruce Armstrong broke down and cried, exclaiming, "Is this the end?" I comforted him and told him I'll find a way to resume circuit working (sic) using manual equipment. I spoke to senior technician Louis Le Mercier who told me he could start up and establish the ship-watch circuit but the working circuit cable terminal will have to be taken from its existing position and transferred and connected to the equipment on the ship-watch circuit. I told him I could do that and promptly did it while he was setting up the necessary equipment. Within minutes we made contact with Banjoewangi by slow speed hand sending and established a working circuit with Banjoewangi relay station, who agreed to receive our traffic for re-processing and re-transmission to destination stations. So we got cracking again, taking turns to do the hand-sending on the recorder keys which was slow and laborious. We got ourselves organised and continued to accept Government and press messages for onward transmission.

That evening, the teleprinter circuit to the Military Command Centre at Fort Canning went dead. The line appeared to have been interrupted. Messages were brought to and fetched from us by dlrs (despatch riders).[31]

It was clear that Donough and his team were now flouting the instructions to deny the enemy access to all vital equipment. However, the need to make sure that Fort Canning still had a line out to the British forces in Java and that remaining Government signals were sent out, made Donough stay at his post despite the heavy shelling and fear that Japanese soldiers would capture them at any moment.

By 15 February, the situation looked hopeless and the team at the C&W were in fear for their lives. If caught by the Japanese, they would surely be executed for assisting the enemy in sending out military signals:

> ...It became apparent that the battle for Singapore would soon end. All messages on hand were cleared. In the evening, after transmitting the last communiqué on General Percival's intended surrender to the Japanese commander on 15 February, we advised Head Office, through Banjoewangi that we were closing down. As a final gesture, we asked the members of the military forces who were taking shelter in the building to come up and write out their last messages to their loved ones and we would have them transmitted. This they did with deep emotion. We sent these messages off and closed down the circuit, leaving Mercier to dismantle the equipment. We then buzzed off before the Japanese soldier got us.[32]

For the rest of the War and for more than 50 years after the end of the Second World War, no one knew of these courageous few men, who risked their lives to keep open Singapore's last communication link with the free world as Japanese troops were less than a mile away.[A]

On the morning of Sunday, 15 February, Japanese troops finally broke through the north of the city as the defending troops along the south coast were retreating.

So it was at 9:30 am that General Percival and his senior commanders met at a Commander's Conference in the Commander, Anti-Aircraft Defence Room, in the Battlebox, to discuss the "tactical situation and any other matters which might be raised". [33]

Present at the meeting were Heath, Bennett, Simmons, Wildey and Simson as well as Brigadier Goodman, Brigadier Royal Artillery; Brigadier Torrance, Brigadier General Staff; Brigadier Lucas, Brigadier in charge of Administration; Brigadier Newbigging, Deputy Adjutant General; Inspector General of Police Dickinson and III Indian Corps interpreter Major Wild.

Percival asked the formation commanders to report on the tactical situation in their respective areas.

All the commanders reported that there had been no major change in the situation since the previous day. There had, however, been some infiltration on the front of the 18th Division (a position west of Adam Road).

Percival then said he regretted to inform the conference that the administrative situation was less satisfactory. He also noted that although the Woodleigh and Mackenzie water pumping stations were still working, there was still very heavy wastage from broken mains and pipes. As a result, the supply in the Fort Canning Reservoir had fallen from 12 million gallons to 2 million gallons since the previous day and fallwould be drained within the next hour or so.

Simson had reported that he gave the whole thing another 24 hours. In response to queries, he repeated that the water position was critical, that the rate of breakage of mains and pipes exceeded repair and that the meagre water supply still available could not now be guaranteed for more than 24 hours and that if a failure took place, it would take several days to obtain piped water again.

The commanders then began to discuss methods on how to economise water and of storing it in receptacles for the use of troops. The Japanese were now in complete control of the Pierce and MacRitchie reservoirs, although water was still flowing to the pumping stations. However, the Woodleigh Pumping Station was now within a few hundred yards of the enemy's forward troops.

Percival also noted that food reserves had now been reduced to about two days, though there were large quantities in the Bukit Timah and Race Course depots which were in enemy hands.

Touching on ammunition, Percival noted there were still adequate reserves of small arms ammunition as there were 4 million rounds in the Fort Canning magazine. However, all the available 25-pounder ammunition had already been issued and there were only 200 boxes of Bofors ammunition (Anti-Aircraft) left while mortar shells were also very short.

The commanders then gave an estimate of what ammunition was likely to be in the forward echelons and methods of economising ammunition were discussed. Only enemy forces of company strength or more would be engaged by artillery fire and only really low-flying aircraft should be engaged by the Anti-Aircraft Artillery, though it was agreed that it was difficult to restrain the gunners from firing at anything within reach.

On the petrol front, it was reported that the only petrol which remained apart from a small dump on the polo ground was what was in vehicle tanks. The commanders agreed to review the list of vehicles in use in order to keep as many off the road and so increase petrol reserves.

It was now that the meeting began to get tense as Percival asked the commanders on their views as to the best course to adopt.

Heath, who had been quiet for a while then weighed in. "In my opinion there us only one possible course to adopt and that is to do what you ought to have done two days ago, namely to surrender immediately," [34] he said. Heath then went on to express his view on the danger of relying on the numberless pools of water where leakage had filled bomb and shell craters as the chief source of water supply for the troops and residents saying a very serious situation would arise if his troops were left without water.

Heath noted now that there was no longer any Bofors ammunition left, the Japanese could come and bomb any target they liked with little or no opposition.

Visibly weary, Heath said there was no way to think they would be able to resist another determined Japanese attack and to sacrifice countless lives by failing to appreciate the situation would be an act of extreme folly. He ended by urging immediate surrender.

Gordon Bennett, the Australian commander agreed with Heath.

Percival then said it was Wavell's order that they should continue to struggle at all cost and without consideration to what may happen to the civil population. "It is our duty to continue fighting as long as we can", he said.[35]

To this Heath replied, "How can General Wavell command this battle from Java?" [36]

It was then that Percival mentioned the counterattack. "I have been considering the possibility of launching a counter-attack shortly, the first object of which would be the recapture of our food depots in the Bukit Timah area. Is this not possible?" [37]

Bennett burst out, asking, "How do you think you are going to maintain the troops if you did get them there? It's quite impracticable", as Heath agreed with his Australian colleague.[38]

Asked for their views, General Simmons said that though he was reluctant to surrender, he could see no alternative.

Most of the other participants remained silent or agreed with surrendering. "There was no dissentient voice".[39]

With Wavell's "discretion to cease resistance" signal already in his pocket, Percival then "in view of the critical water situation and the unsatisfactory administrative situation generally, thereupon reluctantly decided to accept the advice of the senior officers present and to capitulate".[40]

Heath urged that no time be wasted in putting the decision into effect as the negotiations might take some time and that they should be concluded that day.

The conference then decided to send Brigadier Newbigging and the Colonial Secretary as well as an interpreter to meet the Japanese and invite a delegation to visit to Singapore to discuss terms.

On the time of surrender, it was decided that Percival would request a cessation of hostilities from 4:30pm (GMT) and he made it clear, however, that hostilities should continue until definite orders to cease fire were issued.

Discussing what to do about weapons and ordnance, the commanders agreed that weapons would not be destroyed pending the issue of further orders but that orders should be issued for the destruction before 4:30pm of all secret and technical equipment, ciphers, codes and secret documents.

The conference ended at 11:15am (Malayan time) and with that the events of the Ford motor factory followed, leading to the ending of hostilities. A three-man deputation went to Bukit Timah Road at 2pm, where negotiations with Lieutenant Colonel Sugita, Yamashita's staff officer took place.

Instructed to raise a Japanese flag above the Cathay building, the tallest building then, the deputation left after agreeing to a meeting later that day at about 4pm. After the deputation had returned to Fort Canning, Percival along with Brigadier Torrance, Brigadier Newbigging and Major Wild, made their way to the Bukit Timah Rd to be met by Sugita and were brought to the Ford Motor Factory at about 5:15pm.

Percival arrives at the Ford Motor Factory in Bukit Timah in the late afternoon of 15 February 1942 to surrender Singapore. From left to right: Major C.H.D. Wild, Staff Officer 3rd Indian Corps (interpreter), Brigadier T.K. Newbigging, Chief Administration Officer, Colonel Sugita, Intelligence staff officer to General Yamashita, Japanese soldier, Brigadier K.S. Torrance, Brigadier General Staff, Malaya Command and Lieutenant General Arthur E. Percival, General Officer Commanding, Malaya Command.

It was here that Percival met Yamashita for the first time. Percival tried to stall for time but Yamashita demanded an immediate unconditional surrender or a massive assault on the city would follow. Percival caved in and signed the surrender document at about 6:10pm.

With that the Malayan Campaign came to an end in 70 days.

At about 7pm, Torrance came to the Operations Room and drafted an order for the cease-fire to go out at 2000 hours. The order was issued in the name of Simmons, the Fortress Commander:

> Fire will cease at 2030hrs tonight 15/16 Feb 42. Troops will remain in present positions. No movement without permission this HQ. There will NOT repeat NOT be any destruction of arms, equipment maps or records.[41]

Percival signs the surrender document at the Ford Motor Factory in Bukit Timah. On the table is a Japanese-English dictionary brought along by Major Wild, the interpreter. General Tomoyuki Yamashita, Commander of the Japanese forces is seated at the extreme left of the photograph.

There was some confusion as to who was to sign this last order. Finally, it was handed to a Major Waller, who put in an additional line, "all arms and amn (*sic*) to be collected as far as possible", before he signed it. Arms were collected and piled in the entrance porch. The Japanese did not appear.

Percival, who remained listless the whole evening, then went over to the signals office and sent out the last communiqué to troops from Headquarters Malaya Command:

> "It has been necessary to give up the struggle but I want the reason explained to all ranks. The forward troops continue to hold their ground but the essentials of war have run short. In a few days we shall have neither petrol nor food. Many types of ammunition are short and the water supply, upon which the vast civil population and many of the fighting troops are dependent, threatens to fail. This situation has been brought about partly by being driven off our dumps and partly by hostile air and artillery action. Without these sinews of war we cannot fight on. I thank all ranks for their efforts throughout the campaign." [42]

For the rest of the evening, the signal circuits continued to relay lists of names of troops who were on Singapore Island and presumed captured, before dismantling the connections to the outside world.

> ...I was told by another officer that he had heard we were about to surrender. Early that evening a dead silence enveloped the old fort. In the signals rooms, everybody went to sleep, depression and exhaustion flooding in, as we collapsed on mattresses laid on top of cables and land lines. The spring of tension that had kept us going for weeks had been broken.[43]

Endnotes

A After the War, Donough was afraid to mention their bravery as it was an act of defiance of company and military regulations, an offence for which they could be charged. In the mid 1990s, Donough and Barth finally revealed their role in keeping Singapore's communication lines open. However, most of the individuals involved were dead by then and all records of the event were destroyed when Singapore fell to the Japanese on 15 February 1945. Although many listened to Donough's story, none knew whether it was true or the figment of an old man's imagination. Donough told me his story in late 2004 and it rang a bell. When I was looking through the files at the Imperial War Museum a few years back, I came across a miscellaneous cable and wireless document filed in the archive, which I had copied and kept for future reference. I now went back to the document. It was dated 15 February 1942 and was on the letterhead of the South West Pacific Command Java. It was addressed to a Major Kistner at General Headquarters in Bandoeng (Wavell's Headquarters) and was titled, Last Communique from Singapore. In it, the Manager of the Eastern Wireless Service in Java, had listed the details of the last messages from Cable and Wireless in Singapore. It confirmed Donough story that C&W was still operating on 15 February and that the C&W Singapore had sent the fateful signal that Singapore had surrendered. It also listed the personal messages of the soldiers it had forwarded on that fateful day. The final message from Singapore read, "Suggest you stand by in case anything comes from G.O.C. stop Anything further definitely ignore goodbye and good luck stop" Donough had clearly been there when these last messages were sent and his story was obviously true. He and his colleagues have never been recognised for their bravery and for the decision to get the job done despite overwhelming odds. The full communiqué is in the Appendix.

1   *21404 Cipher 27/7, 31189.118/Malaya/207, 27 July 1941, AIR2/1603.* The National Archives, London.

2   *WAR DIARY, Singapore Fortress Signals, December 1941, WO172/156.* The National Archives, London.

3   Ibid

4   *ORGANISATION AND EVOLUTION OF JAPANESE NAVAL SIGINT, PART VI, HW50/59.* The National Archives, London.

5   Ibid, p. 2.

6   *TABLE TALK—ARTHUR COOPER, ORGANISATION AND EVOLUTION OF JAPANESE NAVAL SIGINT, PART VI, HW50/59.* The National Archives, London, p. 2.

7   *ORGANISATION AND EVOLUTION OF JAPANESE NAVAL SIGINT, PART VI, HW50/59.* The National Archives, London, p. 4.

8   *ORGANISATION AND EVOLUTION OF JAPANESE NAVAL SIGINT, PART VI, HW50/59.* The National Archives, London.

9   Wilson, Duncan. *Survival was for Me.* Wigtown, GC Books, 1991. p. 40.

10 *WAR DIARY, Singapore Fortress Signals, December 1941, WO172/156.* The National Archives, London.

11 Ibid

12 Percival, A.E. *The War in Malaya*. Eyre & Spottiswoode, London, 1949. p.185.

13 Ibid

14 Elphick, Peter. *Odd Man Out: The Story of the Singapore Traitor*. Hodder & Stoughton, London. 1993.

15 *ORGANISATION AND EVOLUTION OF JAPANESE NAVAL SIGINT, PART VI, HW50/59.* The National Archives, London, p. 3.

16 *Loss of Singapore Feb 1942 and its lessons for NID, ORGANISATION AND EVOLUTION OF JAPANESE NAVAL SIGINT, PART VI, HW50/59.* The National Archives, London.

17 *ORGANISATION AND EVOLUTION OF JAPANESE NAVAL SIGINT, PART VI, HW50/59.* The National Archives, London.

18 Ibid

19 Percival, A.E. *The War in Malaya*. Eyre & Spottiswoode, London, 1949. p.278.

20 Ibid

21 Lomax, Eric. *The Railway Man*. Vintage, London, 1996. p. 68.

22 Churchill, W.S. *The Second World War: The Hinge of Fate*. Houghton Mifflin Company, Boston, USA, 1950. p. 100.

23 *Order of the Day, 10 February 1942, Papers of A.E. Percival*, P16-27. The Imperial War Museum, London.

24 *FORTRESS COMMAND: INDIAN CORPS: A.I.F.: SOUTHERN AREA, 11 February 1942, P16-27.* The Imperial War Museum, London.

25 *Copley, David. Personal Account, The Battlebox : Research Clippings.* Oral History Department, Singapore.

26 *The Atrocity at Alexandra Hospital, Singapore 14/2/42, Papers of Lieutenant S.E. Bell, 88/63/1.* The Imperial War Museum, London.

27 *Proceedings of the Conference held at Headquarters Malaya Command (Fort Canning) at 1400Hrs. Fri. 13 February 1942, P16-27.* The Imperial War Museum, London.

28 Churchill, W.S. *The Second World War: The Hinge of Fate*. Houghton Mifflin Company, Boston, USA, 1950. p. 105.

29 Ibid

30 Donough, C.O., *Events leading to Fall of Singapore on 15 Feb 42 (9.2.42 to 14.2.42)*. Copy of manuscript with Author, 1998. Interview in September 2004.

31 Ibid, p. 9.

32 Ibid, p. 9.

33 *Proceedings of the Conference held at Headquarters Malaya Command (Fort Canning) at 0930Hrs. Sun. 15 February 1942, Papers of A.E. Percival, P16-27*. The Imperial War Museum, London.

34 Ibid, p.2.

35 Ibid, p.3.

36 Ibid, p. 4.

37 Ibid, p. 4.

38 Ibid, p. 4.

39 Ibid, p. 4.

40 Ibid, p. 4.

41 *Signal, 15 February 1942, Papers of Lieutenant Colonel TH Newey, 85/50/1*. The Imperial War Museum, London.

42 *Signal, 15 February 1942, Papers of A.E. Percival, P16-27*. The Imperial War Museum, London.

43 Lomax, Eric. *The Railway Man*. Vintage, London, 1996. p. 69.

Chapter 6

Occupation and Post War

On the morning of Monday, 16 February, 1942, Chinese New Year's Day, the victorious Japanese Army marched into Singapore town.

Pre-arranged units moved about the city and into Fort Canning where weary Allied headquarters troops awaited them.

Signal officers like Eric Lomax had slept on the floor of the bunker for more than 10 hours after the ceasefire the previous day:

> The following morning I stepped outside and saw four cars moving slowly up the hill, small rising sun pennants fluttering on their wings. Their occupants sat bolt upright, arms stiff by their sides. They drew up outside the main entrance and a group of Japanese officers got out, long swords in black scabbards hanging from their dark green uniforms. They were the first Japanese troops I had ever seen. They strode confidently into the Fort.
>
> These people now ruled Malaya, dominated the seas from India to Polynesia and had broken the power of at least three European empires in Asia. I was their prisoner.[1]

The defeated Allied forces continued to occupy Fort Canning for the next few weeks, as soldiers and officers who were being marched off to Changi and some of whom were being used for clearance works in the city, continued to take supplies from the Command HQ's stores and used the above-ground barracks as shelter until all Allied troops were permanently removed to Changi.

However, by the evening of 18 February, the main buildings at Fort Canning had been taken over as the Defence Headquarters by Major General Saburo Kawamura, the Japanese Commandant of Singapore while General Yamashita was encamped in Bukit Timah.

Under the command of the Defence Headquarters were the Kempeitai, the Japanese military intelligence and security unit, which was believed to have used rooms in the battlebox as torture chambers before they moved to the Young Man's Christian Association (YMCA).

Ian Ward, in his book, *The Killer They Called A God*, noted that Kawamura held a meeting with his senior commanders Miyamoto and Ichikawa as well as Kempetai deputy Oishi that evening at Fort Canning, where the formal operational order for the screening and the killing of Chinese civilians was passed down.

The order, known as the Sook Ching operation, involved killing and torturing an estimated 25,000 to 50,000 Chinese as a reprisal for their alleged sympathy for the Nationalist and Communist Chinese fighting against the Japanese Army in China.

Throughout the Japanese Occupation, it is believed that most of the rooms in the underground complex were left abandoned while the above ground facilities were used.

Although not much else is known about the Battlebox during this period, there were reports, however, of the signals rooms being used during the occupation for communications.

Jim Howard, an Australian war photographer, parachuted into Singapore, following the Japanese surrender announcement on 15 August. At the time, he held three ranks, a Lieutenant-Colonel in the Army, a Wing Commander in the air force, and a Commander in the Navy.

However, he entered Singapore as a 'civilian' as this arrangement allowed him to move around more easily. Howard landed by parachute on 28 August 1945 and entered the Battlebox one or two days later. Here, he saw Japanese soldiers occupying the signal rooms and using the communications facilities. The rooms nearby were barely furnished and the orderlies room had bunks and were occupied by Japanese guards who also cooked there.

Liberation

Once the war ended and the British returned to Singapore, Fort Canning reverted to being the headquarters for the British military.

Although Lord Louis Mountbatten, Supreme Allied Commander, Southeast Asia used the Cathay building as his headquarters, the Allied Land Forces Southeast Asia immediately began re-occupying Fort Canning. Eventually, it became the Headquarters of the General Officer Commanding, Singapore Base District.

The Battlebox, however, was left empty and had by this time been stripped clean by looters during the last days of the occupation.

As the British Military Administration in Singapore began rebuilding the colony and the returned services began to reorganise on the ground, the Battlebox and its operations rooms were forgotten and left abandoned.

By 1963, with Singapore and Malaysia planning to merge as part of the Federation of Malaysia, the Singapore Base District agreed to move its headquarters out of Fort Canning to the General Headquarters of the Far East Land Forces in Tanglin.[2]

With both countries now on the eve of independence, the British government had agreed to move aside its forces so that local defence units could be raised in the country.

By March 1963, it was already decided to vacate Fort Canning, which would now become home to the 4th Federal Infantry Brigade of the Federation Army in Singapore.[3]

In an exchange of letters between the Singapore and Malayan governments in London during the Malaysia talks for merger, it was determined that Fort Canning would be the base for a Federation army for three years before being released to the Singapore Government for development.

The 4th Brigade would merge with the headquarters staff of the Singapore Military Force and the first and second battalions of the Singapore Infantry Regiment.

The rapid buildup of the brigade included the setting up of an Armed Forces Maintenance Corps and the completion of a new Singapore camp at Ulu Pandan for the 2nd Singapore Infantry Regiment.

On 19 August 1963, The 4th Federal Brigade took command of Fort Canning:

> ...the colourful handover ceremony was watched by officers and ranks of both armies. The salute was taken by Maj-Gen E.A.W. Williams, GOC Singapore Base District and Brigadier P.E.M. Bradley, Commanding 4th Federal Brigade.[4]

When Malaya, Singapore, Sabah and Sarawak gained independence from the UK as the Federation of Malaysia on 31 August 1963, the 4th Brigade was in command at Fort Canning, raising the Malaysian flag over the new federation.

While Singapore was part of Malaysia, there were about 4,000 Malaysian troops attached to the 4thFederal Brigade on the island. These included, at separate periods, both the 6th Royal Malay Regiment and the 9th Royal Malay Regiment.

The brigade remained in Singapore from 1963 till after the separation of Singapore and Malaysia which led to Singapore declaring its independence on 9 August 1965.

Singapore felt threatened from its inception and the need for its own defence force was clear after incidents as outlined by then Prime Minister Lee Kuan Yew in his recent memoirs:

> When Parliament was due to open in December 1965, four months after our separation from Malaysia, Brigadier Syed Mohamed Bin Syed Ahmad Alsagoff, who was in charge of a Malaysian brigade stationed in Singapore (4th Federal Brigade at Fort Canning), called on me and insisted that his motorcycle outriders escort me to Parliament. Alsagoff was a stout, heavy-built Arab Muslim with a moustache, a Singaporean by birth who had joined the Malayan Armed Forces. To my amazement he acted as if he was the commander-in-chief of the army in Singapore, ready at any time to take over control of the island. At that time the First and Second Singapore Infantry regiments (1 and 2 SIR) of about 1,000 men each were under Malaysian command. The Malaysian government had placed 700 Malaysians in 1 and 2 SIR, and posted out 300 Singaporean soldiers to various Malaysian units.
>
> I weighed up the situation and concluded that the Tunku (Tunku Abdul Rahman, the Malaysian Prime Minister) wanted to remind us

and the foreign diplomats who would be present that Malaysia was still in charge in Singapore. If I told him off for his presumptuousness, Alsagoff would report this back to his superiors in Kuala Lumpur and they would take other steps to show me who wielded real power in Singapore. I decided it was best to acquiesce. So for the ceremonial opening of the first Parliament of the Republic of Singapore, Malaysian army outriders "escorted" me from my office in City Hall to Parliament House...

...Shortly after separation, at the request of the Malaysian government, we had sent the 2nd battalion SIR to Sabah for Confrontation duties. We wanted to demonstrate our good faith and solidarity with Malaysia even though a formal defence treaty had not been concluded. This left their barracks, Camp Temasek, vacant. We then agreed to a Malaysian proposal that one Malaysian regiment be sent down to Camp Temasek. The 2nd battalion SIR was due to return from its duties in Borneo in February 1966, and arrangements were made at staff level for the Malaysian regiment to withdraw. The Malaysian defence minister requested that instead of reoccupying Camp Temasek, one Singapore battalion should be sent to the Malayan mainland to enable the Malaysian regiment to remain where it was. Keng Swee (Goh Keng Swee, then Singapore Defence Minister and Deputy Prime Minister) did not agree. We wanted both our own battalions in Singapore. We believed the Malaysians had changed their minds because they wanted to keep one battalion of Malaysian forces in Singapore to control us.

The Malaysians refused to move out, so the SIR advance party had to live under canvas at Farrer Park. Keng Swee saw me urgently to warn that if our troops were under canvas too long, with poor facilities for their mess and toilets, there was the risk of a riot or a mutiny. He compared himself to a British General in charge of troops the majority of whom were Italians. The Malaysians could take advantage of this and, through Brigadier Alsagoff, mount a coup. He advised me to move from my home in Oxley Road into the Istana Villa in the Istana domain and to post Gurkha police guards around just in case. For the next few weeks, my family and I stayed there with a company of Gurkhas on standby.

Shortly afterwards, the British vacated a camp called Khatib in the north of Singapore, near Sembawang. We offered it to the Malaysians and they agreed in mid-March 1966 to move out of our camp to Khatib, where they remained for 18 months before withdrawing of their own accord in November 1967.[5]

*In the post-War period, Fort Canning became the Headquarters of
the Singapore Base District, before it was handed over to the newly
Independent Government of Malaysia for use by Federal Troops in 1963.
In the 1970s, it housed the Singapore Command and Staff College, which
were the last occupants of the above ground buildings before some of
the buildings were restored in the 1980s.*

It would take a few more months more before the Federal Army would vacate Fort Canning and move most of their troops off the island.

Speaking in the Singapore Parliament on 25 January, 1968, Mr Lee announced the final pullout of more than 1,000 troops of the 4th Malaysian Federal Brigade.

> (Lee) told the House that all Malaysian Army units had been withdrawn from Singapore by the end of last year, following a letter from the Malaysian Deputy Prime Minister, Tun Razak, to Singapore's Minister for Defence, Mr. Lim Kim San, on Nov 14. Tun Razak had written to say that as Singapore had increased its armed forces for its own defence, it was no longer necessary to station Malaysian troops in Singapore. ...The last units to leave here were mostly infantrymen and members of the Reconnaissance Corps.[6]

By then, the Malaysian government was only maintaining the Royal Malaysian Navy Base at Woodlands, which remained the headquarters of the Malaysian Navy till the late 1980s with the complete pullout from the Woodlands base in the early 1990s.

Things appeared bleak for Singapore as the British forces, which had promised under an earlier British Government to remain engaged in Singapore till the end of the 1970s, had now decided to pullout of Singapore by 1970/71.

As the British began their massive pullout east of Suez, after the change in political leadership in the UK and a massive defence review, London was persuaded to hand over much of its facilities and equipment to the Singapore government.

The impact of the British move was very significant for an economy that virtually depended on the military presence on the island.

In public talks and discussions, many were concerned with the impact of the move.

> ...It may be that the total unemployed and underemployed in Singapore now amounts to between 50 to 80 thousand. The withdrawal of the British Forces may throw another 100,000 people on the labour market over the withdrawal period... The Finance Minister recently pointed out that in spite of tremendous efforts new jobs had been created only at the rate of 5,000 a year since

1963. The EDB (Economic Development Board) planners calculate that an investment of $25 to $30 thousand is required to create one new job. This means that Singapore will need a total investment of nearly $3,000 million to keep the unemployment rate down to its present level before the British forces withdrawal.

...Obviously the help to be given by Britain must be substantial and in hard cash. It is no use to say that investment from Britain will be encouraged to fill the gap. A businessman invests money because he thinks he will make a profit on the investment, he does not do it out of charity because a British political party (and not even his own political party) has broken promises regarding the military bases...[7]

From 1968 to 1969, the British Government handed over $135 million worth of property to the Singapore government, including the Naval Base worth about $12.7 million at the time.[8] In the end, the British Government handed over more than $400 million worth of fixed and moveable assets to the Singapore Government.[9]

Other properties included the three RAF bases at Changi, Seletar and Tengah, the Far Eastern Land Forces (Farelf) Headquarters at Tanglin as well as the Pasir Panjang complex occupied by the British Army. It also included Flagstaff, Command and Air House as well as several other major residences of British service chiefs in Singapore.

With Fort Canning now empty and the Singapore Armed Forces trying to build up its fledgling defence force, the above ground buildings were handed over to the newly set up Singapore Command and Staff College.

The aims of the SCSC were to prepare senior officers for Staff and Command appointments at Battalion, Formation and Ministry levels and to provide the institutional framework for formulating operational doctrines at the highest levels.

The general education subjects were prepared by Mr Doraisingam S. Samuel, the first General Education Officer of SCSC and later Head of the Education Department at Singapore's Ministry of Defence

Mr Samuel who later became President of the Singapore History Association, was the man who had sent the first letter to the Straits Times in 1988, setting in motion the whole chain of events in the re-discovery of the Battlebox.

Sometime in the late 60s, it was decided to seal off the underground bunkers as it was a security risk so near the college and for fear that people might get lost in the tunnels. The Battlebox was then sealed off till its re-discovery, almost two decades later.

The SCSC remained on Fort Canning till the mid 1970s before it moved to Seletar Camp, leaving the above ground buildings and the bunkers surrounding the former Headquarters Malaya Command empty.

In the mid 1980s, the above ground barracks was restored and converted for use as an arts centre and for cultural events on the slopes of the hill.

In the meantime, the National Parks Department had decided to preserve the Fort Canning buildings and began searching for suitable investors to develop the Battlebox as a museum.

The main above ground building of Headquarters Malaya Command was restored and partially re-developed in the 1990s. In 1993, the National Parks Board gave a 30 year lease of the above ground buildings and the Battlebox to eye-care products firm Alliance Technology and Development for slightly over $51 million.[10]

Its subsidiary, the Fort Canning Country Club Investment Ltd, restored the above ground buildings and converted it into the Fort Canning Country Club.

It spent $3 million restoring the Battlebox and creating a state-of-the-art museum within the walls of the bunker. The Battlebox museum was formally opened on 15 February 1997, fifty-five years to the day Singapore fell. The Battlebox's first curator Tan Teng Teng and military historian Dr Ong Chit Chung carried out extensive research to create a realistic atmosphere in the bunker.[11]

Using special audio and video effects, high-end animatronics and specially crafted figurines, the museum did a very credible job in bringing visitors back to the morning of 15 February 1942. With well-researched displays and interactive installations, the Battlebox had once again been brought back to life, no longer a nerve centre of military forces but more a reminder of how crucial a good headquarters and command staff are to any military operation.

This photograph was taken outside the Battlebox's Dobbie Rise entrance, showing the staircase to the Battlebox from the above ground buildings in the background. These stairs were initially camouflaged and was known only to highly cleared staff of Headquarters Malaya Command. The steps were made of rough stone and was crumbling in 1988. As part of conservation efforts, a new staircase was installed, which is now more accessible and safer. Today, visitors can use the stairs to enter the Legends Fort Canning Park Clubhouse, where they can enjoy refreshments after visiting the museum.

However, the severe financial crisis that hit Southeast Asia in late 1997 meant that the Country Club and museum faced very lean times. By April 2002, Alliance Technology and Development had been placed under judicial management with debts totaling almost $1 billion. In November that year, the families behind cinema operator Eng Wah Organisation and The Legends Gold and Country Resort in Johor bought the struggling club "for just over half of its $15 million asking price".[12] It purchased another 30-year lease from the National Parks Board at $85 million and with significant investments and improving economic times, run the club and museum as a more profitable venture.

The club was re-launched as The Legends Fort Canning Park in November 2002, a town club located in the middle of Fort Canning Park.

General Percival's former headquarters now consists of eight restaurants and bars, a state-of-the-art 10,000 sq ft gym, three swimming pools, a spa, a rest and relax room, a private members' lounge with wireless Internet access, meeting and dining suites, a grand ball room and a children's centre among many other facilities. Members also enjoy membership privileges at The Legends Golf and Country Resort in Johor.

More than 60 years after the end of the Second World War, the Malayan Campaign still remains a key defining moment in the history of Malaysia and Singapore. The battles fought in Malaya and torture and deprivation imposed by Japanese troops are seared in the minds of those who lived through it. For many in my generation, who were born more than 30 years after the War, the stories of elderly relatives and old war veterans have come to shape our collective perception of what happened in those dark days back in 1942.

For many, it is not easy to remember those days much less record them down on paper. As a result, historians today face huge gaps in trying to piece together what actually happened during those 70 days, when the fate of Southeast Asia was determined in the rice paddies and plains of Malaya.

Although this book has attempted to give a clearer picture of the Battlebox and the crucial role it played in those fateful days, it is by no means comprehensive or complete. There are many more secrets and turns to the story that have yet to be revealed. Although most of the highly sensitive files on Singapore have been opened to the public, a few are still sealed by the British Government and will not be declassified till 2045.

Many more stories and details of the Fall of Singapore have been lost with the passing on of those who witnessed the final death throes of the city. Even with the release of all files on the War, we will never get the full picture of the Battlebox. It is a puzzle that brings with it more questions for every answer that it provides. It is hoped that in the coming years, many of those who are still around and who will read this book, will find it in themselves to come forward and give their account of what happened in the Battlebox and in the final hours before the Surrender on that fateful Sunday afternoon, six decades ago.

Endnotes

1 Lomax, Eric. *The Railway Man*. Vintage, London, 1996. p. 70.

2 Yeo, Joseph. *Defence:The big switch has begun, The Sunday Times.*
   3 March 1963.

3 *Takeover without a shot at Fort Canning, The Straits Times.*
   5 March 1963.

4 *Malay Mail*, 20 August 1963.

5 Lee, Kuan Yew. *From Third World to First: The Singapore Story:
   1965-2000*. Times Editions, Singapore. 2000.

6 Pestana, Roderick. *Malaysia pulls last troops out of Singapore, Malay Mail.*
   26 January 1968.

7 Hazell, R.C. *Economic and Social Effects of the British Withdrawal from
   Singapore.* A talk for Rotary West, Singapore, 5 March 1968.

8 Rozario, Francis. *Handover of $135m property, The Straits Times.*
   5 February 1969.

9 *Undated Treasury Minute, 1971 concerning the gift of fixed assets
   and equipment to the Government of Malaysia (Singapore portion),
   WO32/21583.* The National Archives, London.

10 *The Straits Times*, 13 November 2002

11 *The Straits Times*, 15 February 1997

12 *The Straits Times*, 15 November 2002

Appendix

SOUTH WEST PACIFIC COMMAND,
JAVA

15th FEBRUARY, 1942.

LAST COMMUNIQUE FROM SINGAPORE

For Major Kistner General Headquarters BANDOENG.

Following are details of Cable and Wireless
final stand at SINGAPORE stop

1840	Japs have not got us yet, but very near stop We have phone to Fort Canning stop G.O.C. Fort Canning advises us to surrender stop We don't know exactly position stop Office roof shambles and place full dust and smoke stop
2148	We have surrendered Armistice now on stop
2156	Surrender not official and not for publication stop We have been informed fighting has ceased stop
2205	Personal messages from following members Army Signal Staff Giblin Price Flynn Benny Reeves accepted and forwarded by Cable and Wireless Staff stop
2206	Now we off goodbye for present stop
2210	Suggest you stand by in case anything comes from G.O.C. stop Anything further definitely ignore goodbye and good luck stop

Thus the final word from SINGAPORE over the Cable
was at 2211/15th stop All above times S'pore times stop
Please acknowledge

Manager,
EASTERN.

This is the list of last cable messages sent out of Singapore prior to its fall on 15 February 1945. This document verifies C.O. Donough's story of keeping the cable office open right till the bitter end.

A Brief Chronology of Events

1936	War Office approves building of underground command centre at Fort Canning as part of Headquarters Malaya command plan for defence of Malaya. Work begins
1939	Air Ministry approves plan for location of new RAF headquarters in Singapore at Sime Road, work begins
1940	Underground Command Centre at Fort Canning is operational
May 1941	Pecival takes over as General Officer Commanding, Malaya Command
June	Brooke-Popham sanctions immediate work on building of new Army Headquarters and Air Force and Army Combined Operations Room at Sime Road adjacent to RAF Headquarters
1 Dec	*Prince of Wales* and *Repulse* arrive in Singapore
6 Dec	First Degree of Readiness ordered (RAFFLES), new Army headquarters and Combined Operations Room begins operations at Sime Road
7 Dec	FECB warns Brooke-Popham that Japanese invasion on Malaya imminent
8 Dec	Japan attacks Malaya, Thailand, Pearl Harbour and Hong Kong. First air raid over Singapore. Planned Operation Matador (pre-emptive strike into Thailand) abandoned but two small probes made, one codenamed Krohcol, designed to capture the strategic height known as "The ledge" in Southern Thailand
9 Dec	Kuantan airfield abandoned
10 Dec	*Prince of Wales* and *Repulse* sunk off Kuantan
11 Dec	Krohcol column fails to reach "The ledge" and retreats
12 Dec	British forces from Kota Bahru commence retreat down rail line to Kuala Lipis

13 Dec	British forces retreat south of Jitra
15 Dec	Fighting in Gurun, followed by retreat
16 Dec	Penang under seige
17 Dec	Penang evacuated
23 Dec	British withdraw across Perak River
25 Dec	Hong Kong surrenders
30 Dec	First Japanese land attack on Kuantan
30 Dec – 2 Jan	Battle at Kampar followed by further retreat
3 Jan 1942	45th Indian Brigade arrives in Singapore
4 Jan	Allied troops take up position at Slim River
7 Jan	Slim River battle fought. Japanese spearhead attack with tanks and British forces pushed back. Central Malaya now open to Japanese. General Sir Archibald Wavell, new Supreme Allied Commander, South West Pacific, visits Malaya
11 Jan	Japanese march into Kuala Lumpur
13 Jan	53rd British Brigade of 18th Division arrive in Singapore
14 Jan	Australian 8th Division deployed in Johore attack. Successful ambush at Gemas with heavy Japanese loss
15 Jan	Battle at Muar with two battalions of the 45th Indian Brigade broken
19 – 23 Jan	Cut off Australian and Indian troops from Bakri/Yong Peng Area
24 Jan	Australian reinforcements arrive in Singapore
27 Jan	22nd Indian Brigade cut off at Layang Layang and destroyed
30 – 31 Jan	British Forces retreat across the Causeway to Singapore island with Singapore under continuous air attack
5 Feb	Remainder of 18th Division arrives in Singapore
7 Feb	Japanese begin artillery shelling of island
8 Feb	Japanese launch amphibious attack in the evening against Australians

10 Feb	Kranji-Jurong Line lost to Japanese. Wavell makes last visit to Singapore. Damages back when he falls off quay when leaving Singapore and is hospitalised and runs rest of campaign from bed.
11 Feb	Percival moves the Combined Headquarters from Sime Road to the Battlebox at Fort Canning
12 Feb	British retreat to final perimeter around Singapore town
15 Feb	Percival surrenders Singapore, Malayan Campaign ends
18 Feb	Japanese occupy Fort Canning
8 Sep 1945	British re-occupy Fort Canning, becomes Headquarters of Singapore Base District
19 Sep 1963	Malaysian Fourth Federal Infantry Brigade takes over Fort Canning as part of Malaysia merger Agreement
Mar 1966	4th Federal Infantry Brigade pulls out of Fort Canning, complex handed over to the Singapore Armed Forces
Late 1967	The SAF's Singapore Command and Staff College established at Fort Canning
Mid-1975	SCSC vacates Fort Canning for its new premises in Seletar Camp
Mid-1980	Some of the above ground buildings re-furbished as an arts centre
Mid 1990s	Conservation and re-development by the Parks Department and National Heritage Board
15 Feb 1997	Launch of Fort Canning Country Club and the Battlebox Museum
Nov 2002	Launch of Legends Fort Canning Park and the Battlebox Museum

Dramatis Personae

ARMY

General Sir Archibald Wavell	Supreme Commander, South West Pacific Command/Comander, ABDA Command
Lieutenant General Arthur E. Percival	General Officer Commanding, Headquarters Malaya Command
Lieutenant General Sir Lewis Heath	General Officer Commanding, III Indian Corps
Major General Gordon Bennett	Commander, 8th Australian Division
Major General F. Keith Simmons	Commander, Singapore Fortress
Brigadier A.D. Curtiss	Commander, Fixed Defences
Brigadier T K Newbigging	Chief Administration Officer
Brigader Ivan Simson	Chief Engineer, Malaya Command
Brigadier K.S. Torrance	Brigadier General Staff, Malaya Command
Brigadier A.W.G. Wildey	Commander, Anti-Aircraft Defences
Lieutenant-Col C.C.M. Macleod-Carey	Deputy Commander 7th Coast Artillery Regiment
Major Hugh-Lindley Jones	Gun Control Officer, the Battlebox
Major C.H.D. Wild	Staff Officer, III Indian Corps
Eric Lomax	Signaler, Malaya Command

AIR FORCE

Air Marshal Sir Robert Brooke-Popham	Commander-in-Chief, Far East
Air Vice Marshal C.W.H. Pulford	Air Officer Commanding, RAF Far East

NAVY

Admiral Sir Tom Phillips	Commander, Force Z (*HMS Prince of Wales* and *Repulse*)
Vice-Admiral Sir Geoffrey Layton	Commander-in-Chief, China Fleet
Lieutenant Commander David Copley	Secretary to Extended Defence Officer, the Battlebox
Ray Stubbs	Royal Navy Coder, the Battlebox

JAPANESE

Lieutenant General Tomoyuki Yamashita	Commander of Japanese forces in Malayan Campaign
Major General Takuma Nishimura	Commander, Imperial Guards Division
Major General Saburo Kawamura	Japanese Commandant of Singapore

OTHERS

Sir Shenton Whitlegge Thomas	Governor of Singapore, 1935-1942
Sir Stamford Raffles	Founder of Singapore
Cuthbert Oswald Donough	Operator, Cable & Wireless, Singapore
Lee Kuan Yew	First Prime Minister of Singapore
Goh Keng Swee	Then Singapore Deputy Prime Minister and Defence Minister
Doraisingam S. Samuel	President, Singapore History Association
Felix Soh	Associate News Editor, The Straits Times (1988)
Tunku Abdul Rahman	First Prime Minister of Malaysia
Brigadier Syed Mohamed Bin Syed Alsagoff	Commander, 4th Federal Brigade

BIBLIOGRAPHY

Primary Sources

The National Archives (Public Records Office), London

AIR2   Air Ministry Papers, Far East, Accomodation, 1930-1942

ADM1   Admiralty: Real Estate, Far East, 1968-1972

CAB65   War Cabinet: Minutes, 1939-1945

CAB66   War Cabinet: Memoranda, WP and CP series, 1939-1945

CAB79   War Cabinet: Chiefs of Staff Committee Minutes, 1939-1945

CAB80   War Cabinet: Chiefs of Staff Committee Memoranda, 1939-1945

CAB94   War Cabinet: Overseas Defence Committee, 1939-1942

CAB100 War Cabinet: Daily Situation Reports, 1939-1942

CAB105 War Cabinet:Telegrams, 1941-1948

HW50   Far Eastern Combined Bureau, 1936-1945

OD39   Ministry of Overseas Development and Overseas Development Administration: Malaysia and Singapore Department and successors,1966 to1973

WO32   Disposal of Real Estate, 1970-1975

WO172   Malaya Command Papers, 1939-1942

WO203   Military Headquarters Papers, Far East Forces, 1941-1945

WO216   Chief of Imperial General Staff Papers, 1935-1942

Imperial War Museum, London

Carter, Wing Commander T.C., Papers

Cazalet, Vice-Admiral Sir Peter, Papers

Heath, Lt Gen Sir Lewis, Papers

Kirby, Lt Col S.W., Notes on Singapore, 1936

Percival, Lt Gen A.E., Papers

Simpson-Oliver, 2nd Lt E., Papers

Thomas, Governor Sir T.S.W., Communique, Feb 16, 1942

Wild, Lt Col C.H.D., Notes on the Malayan Campaign,
Notes on the Capitulation of Singapore

National Army Museum, London

Deakin, Lt Col C.C., and Webb, Maj G.M.S., 5th Battalion/2nd Punjab
Regiment Papers

Frith, Lt Col The Rev John, 2nd Baluch regiment – Malaya
Campaign Notes 1939 – 15 Feb 1942

Jones, Col J.L., Papers

Kelling, G.H., British and local forces in Malaya 1786-1945,
unpublished Thesis, 1981

Macleod-Carey, Lt Col C.C.M., *Singapore Guns, War Monthly*,
Issue 34, pgs 34-39

Malaya Command, Tactical Notes for Malaya 1940: Issued by the
General Staff, Malaya Command, reprinted by General Staff,
India, 1941

Others

Author Interview with C.O. Donough, 2 September 2004

Research Clippings on the Battlebox, Oral History Department, Singapore

Secondary Sources

Despatches

Brooke-Popham, Air Chief Marshall Sir Robert, Commander-in-Chief in the Far East, Operations in the Far East from 17 October 1940 to 27 December 1941, H.M.S.O., 1948

Percival, Lt. Gen A.E., Operations of Malaya Command, from 8 December 1941 to 15 February, 1942, H.M.S.O., 1948

Wavell, General A.P., Despatch by the Supreme Commander of the A.B.D.A. area to the Combined Chiefs of Staff on the operations in the South-West Pacific from 15 January 1942 to 25 February 1942, H.M.S.O., 1948

Books

Attiwell, Kenneth, *The Singapore Story*. New York: Doubleday, 1960

Barber, Noel, *A Sinister Twilight: The Fall of Singapore 1942*. Boston: Houghton Mifflin, 1968

Bennett, H. Gordon, *Why Singapore Fell*. Sydney: Angus & Robertson, Ltd., 1944

Braddon, Russell, *The Naked Island*. London: Werner Laurie, 1952

Brown, Cecil, *Suez to Singapore*. New York: Random House, 1942

Chapman, F. Spencer, *The Jungle is Neutral*. Singapore: Times Editions-Marshall Cavendish, reprinted 2005

Chin Kee Onn, *Malaya Upside Down*. Singapore: Jitts, 1946

Churchill, Winston S., *The Second World War. Vol 4 The Hinge of Fate*. Boston: Houghton Mifflin, 1950

Cooper, A. Duff, Old Men Forget. New York: Dutton 1954

Donahue, Arthur G., *Last Flight from Singapore*. London: Macmillan, 1944

Falk, Stanley, *Seventy Days to Singapore*. New York: G.P. Putnam's Sons, 1975

Gallagher, O.D., *Action in the East*. London: George G. Harrap, 1942

Grenfell, Russell, *Main Fleet to Singapore*. London: Faber & Faber Ltd, 1951

Kirby, S.W., *Singapore: The Chain of Disaster*. New York: Macmillan, 1971

Low, N.I., *When Singapore was Syonan-To*. Singapore: Times Editions, reprinted 2004

Mant, Gilbert, *Grim Glory*. Sydney: Currawong, 1945

Morrison, Ian, *Malayan Postscript*. Faber & Faber, 1943

Owen, Frank, *The Fall of Singapore*. London: Michael Joseph, 1960

Percival, A.E. *The War in Malaya*. London: Eyre & Spottiswoode, 1949

Simson, Ivan, *Singapore: Too Little, Too Late*. London: Leo Cooper Ltd, 1970

Tsuji, Masanobu, *Singapore: The Japanese Version*. Translated by M.E. Lake. New York: St. Martin's Press, 1960

Smyth, John., *V.C. Percival and the Tragedy of Singapore*. London: Macdonald, 1971

Articles

Bose, Romen, *Percival's Last Stand. The Straits Times*, 26 July 1988

Canning as National Preserves. The Malay Mail, 20 February 1969

Farming plans for Naval Base land. The Straits Times, 1 August 1963

Malaysian Army takes over Fort Canning. The Malay Mail, 18 Sept. 1963

Pestana, Roderick, *Malaysia pulls last troops out of Singapore. The Straits Times*, 26 January 1968

Rozario, Francis, *Handover of $135m Property. The Straits Times*, 5 February 1969

Sam, Jackie, *Federation Army to use Fort Canning as Base. The Sunday Times*, 28 July 1963

See, Constance, *Historic Command House up for rent at $30,000 a month*. Home, *The Straits Times*, 4 April 1993

Takeover without a shot at Fort Canning. The Straits Times, 5 March 1963

Thousand acres of WD land for Singapore. The Straits Times, 9 July 1963

Yeo, Geraldine, *Lion City Memories.* Life!, The Straits Times, 11 March 1999

Yeo, Joseph, *Defence: The big switch has begun.* The Sunday Times,
3 March 1963

About the Author

A senior journalist with international news organisation Agence France-Presse (AFP), Romen Bose has written extensively on the Second World War in Singapore and has been involved in researching Singapore and the region's military history for the last two decades. His books include, *The End of the War: Singapore's Liberation and the aftermath of the Second World War*; *Kranji: The Commonwealth War Cemetery and the Politics of the Dead*; *Fortress Singapore: A Battlefield Guide* and *A Will for Freedom: The Indian Independence Movement in Southeast Asia*. He and his wife Brigid have three daughters Lara, Olive and Cilla.